I0823592

STRAIGHT FROM THE GRAPEVINE

STRAIGHT FROM THE GRAPEVINE

HOW TO CRUSH YOUR JOB SEARCH

YOUR STARTER PACK FOR CAREER SUCCESS

RACHEL ZASLANSKY SHEER

& LORI ZUKER BRILLER

A POST HILL PRESS BOOK
ISBN: 979-8-89565-475-0
ISBN (eBook): 979-8-89565-476-7

Straight from the Grapevine:
How to Crush Your Job Search

Cover design by Conroy Accord

Post Hill Press
New York • Nashville
posthillpress.com

Published in the United States of America
1 2 3 4 5 6 7 8 9 10

To Hazel Sheer, Griffin Sheer, Addison Briller, and Sascha Briller:

Our greatest hope is that we've inspired you to work hard, follow your passions, and define success on your own terms. May you always strive to be kind, curious, and good people above all else. When the time comes to begin your own career journeys, we hope this book serves as your trusted guide to help you navigate the job search with confidence, purpose, and heart.

We love you.

TABLE OF CONTENTS

INTRODUCTION

If you're reading this, you're probably starting the journey of finding your place in the working world. And while the interview process can feel overwhelming (because it is), take a deep breath. You found us just in time. Welcome to the ultimate playbook for mastering your job search and landing the right job. We've seen the mistakes. (All of them.) But we took notes so you don't have to repeat them.

This process can be easy if you follow our lead. We got you.

Who Are We?

We're Lori and Rachel, two ambitious New Yorkers who landed in Los Angeles to work in entertainment. We never imagined our paths would cross, let alone lead to a twenty-year business partnership. Together, we co-founded Grapevine—a staffing firm specializing in placing top-tier support for high-end clients. We like to think of ourselves as expert job matchmakers.

Not to age ourselves, but pre-LinkedIn, there was no clear path connecting job seekers to employers. So…we built one.

Sure, a few traditional staffing agencies existed, but none felt fresh or aligned with the fast-moving, digitally driven world we suddenly found ourselves in. So, we launched our own…with a more modern spin.

We began by collecting emails from our network—friends, colleagues, assistants, agents, you name it—and sending out weekly job lists featuring every role we were working on. It spread like wildfire. We were ahead of the curve, and people noticed. Before long, our resource became the go-to, referral-only list for jobs in entertainment and lifestyle.

The response was immediate. We got daily calls and emails from people asking to be added to the list. For years, we were the only ones doing it and it completely shifted how people searched for jobs in our industry. Our weekly job lists set us apart and made job hunting feel exciting again.

Fast-forward twenty years: We've built a reputation for helping people land dream jobs and coaching the next generation to do the same. What keeps people coming back to us—time and time again—isn't just the wins. It's the tough love, the spot-on matches, and the trust we've earned along the way.

We specialize in placing top-tier assistants and staff with high-profile clients, celebrities, athletes, fortune 500 executives, and beyond.

One thing we know for sure: Preparing for the job market isn't as hard as it seems…*if* you know the right steps to take. Follow our lead, and watch the doors start to open.

Meet Lori Zuker Briller

I'm your typical Upper East Sider, but instead of staying in the familiar bubble of New York City, I decided to mix things up and head to the University of Wisconsin for college. It was quieter, friendlier, and surprisingly refreshing—a complete shift from the polish of Manhattan.

That decision sparked a path full of unexpected turns for me: countless internships, a life-changing backpacking trip abroad, and eventually, a leap into the heart of Hollywood. I've had the privilege of working at powerhouse companies like CNN, Turner, Will Smith's Overbrook Entertainment, and Alec Baldwin's production company, El Dorado Pictures.

But life has a way of surprising you. After years in production, I pivoted and spent several years as a recruiter, helping others find their place in the entertainment industry. Every chapter of my career has taught me something new. If there's one thing I've learned, it's this: Every experience matters. Find what lights you up, trust the journey, and always stay true to who you are. And then I met Rachel, who is now my work wife of twenty years.

Meet Rachel Zaslansky Sheer

I grew up in a New York suburb, in a town where most people followed a fairly traditional path. But I was always interested in writing my own story. I headed to the University of Maryland, where I studied psychology with a concentration in women's studies, and worked every job under the sun. Bagels, ice cream, smoothies…I basically covered the entire food pyramid while figuring out who I was, and what I wanted.

After college—with no job and very little savings—I decided to take a leap of faith and move to Los Angeles, following some likeminded friends. The entirety of my life's legacy was crammed into eight large brown boxes. Since I cheaped out and shipped them without any tracking, naturally they never arrived. Clean slate. All I had were some suitcases and a gut feeling that LA was where I was meant to be. After a few months of living it up (and maxing out my first credit card), I landed a job at Creative Artists Agency (CAA) working for two junior talent agents.

It was fast-paced, intense, and definitely a crash course in the entertainment industry. After a year, I was pulled up to one of the managing partner's desks, where I spent the next couple years running at full speed and learning a ton.

Deep down, I knew being an agent wasn't for me. So I tried something different and became an executive assistant at a production company, supporting two producers. I thought maybe this would be the sweet spot; instead, it left me feeling burnt out and disillusioned. Turns out, the dream I thought I was chasing didn't quite match the reality.

I realized I didn't have to force myself into a mold that didn't fit. I had built an amazing network. I had strong relationships across the industry, and I naturally found myself connecting people in my network with jobs. That's when the light bulb went off.

I've always had the entrepreneurial bug. My dad is a business owner, and I knew I wanted to be a boss like him. But in what? I had no idea! I started sketching out my own vision. I didn't have a business plan, because quite frankly, I didn't know what one was yet. I certainly didn't have any investors—all of my relationships were with assistants at that time. But I had a laptop, a lot of hustle, and a belief that I could create a better system for people looking for new jobs. Finally in June of 2005, Grapevine was born.

How Our Worlds Collided—The Coffee Bean Moment

Rachel:

"Here's the twist in our story: We didn't meet at some grand networking event or through any sort of formal industry connections. It was quite the opposite. At the time, I was freshly out of a job and had the idea to utilize my entertainment network by starting a staffing agency out of my very glamorous office (aka my dining room). Very early on, my phone rang with an unknown number, which I naturally let go to voicemail. I received a message from a woman named Lori telling me that she heard I was creating a new staffing agency, and she wanted to be my partner?! I had so many thoughts all at once. Who is this woman with balls of steel calling me out of the blue with such a presumptuous idea, and how am I going to get out of this? Can I just ignore the message? Curiosity finally set in and I actually called her back."

Lori: (laughing)

"Whatever!! A friend of mine had told me about Rachel and what she had been planning, and it was like, what do I have to lose? I did what I do best, and researched. I found her number and literally just called her. I decided to shoot my shot. I knew it was bold, but at that point I just had to listen to my gut and make the call. I don't remember asking to be your partner in the message, but your memory is better than mine. I knew it was weird, but what was the worst thing that could happen—you hung up on me? You said no? So what? I made the call, and you agreed to meet me."

Rachel:

"I kind of felt bad for her, which is why I agreed to take the meeting. She just sounded so determined. I will admit her offer did pique my interest. We met at the Coffee Bean in Beverly Hills because it was nice and close to my apartment. In my mind, this was a quick thirty-minute coffee—in and out—and back on with the rest of my day."

Lori:

"I think I was nervous, but I was on a mission."

Rachel:

"I was just trying to figure out how to let her down gently and quickly. We wound up chatting about our industry relationships and our experiences with staffing people in jobs and our NY connection. Once I let my guard down, I realized we actually had a lot in common—most importantly, a shared goal. She was persistent and sharp and had so many great ideas that she literally brought to that Coffee Bean table. Cut to an hour later, we shook hands, and I left the Coffee Bean with a total stranger as my business partner! No contract, no looking back."

Lori: "You're welcome!"

And here we are, twenty years later. We're writing this book because we've seen it all, and we want to share everything we've learned along the way. We've built our company from the ground up, weathered plenty of storms, and worked with some of the most successful and powerful people in the world. But we're not here to brag; we're here to give you the tools, the guidance, and the insight to crush your own job search!

This book will empower you to nail the interview process and land the job. In each chapter, we've included five key takeaways that you can immediately apply to your job search. Think of it as your personal guide to success.

Five Takeaways to the First Taste

1. **Take the Meeting:** Opportunities don't always come in the form you expect. Be open to the unexpected.
2. **Make the Cold Call:** Sometimes, it's the bold moves that lead to the best opportunities.
3. **Dream Big and Live Outside the Lines:** Don't limit yourself to what you think is possible. Shoot for the stars!
4. **Look for the Signs:** Trust your instincts. There are opportunities all around you, if you're tuned in.
5. **Be Persistent:** Even when things seem uncertain, keep pushing forward and believe in yourself.

CHAPTER 1

PLANTING THE SEEDLINGS—IT'S NEVER TOO EARLY

Let's not waste any time—your future career starts right now. Students in high school and even college often think they have plenty of time before they need to think about their professional futures. But the truth is, the earlier you start building your career game plan, the better prepared you'll be when it's time to start the job hunt. Think of this chapter as your playbook to laying the groundwork for your future job search, no matter what path you decide to take.

Start Early—In Your Own Backyard

Babysitting. Dog walking. Serving popcorn at the movie theater. Your first job doesn't have to be glamorous—it just needs to teach you how to show up, how to follow through, and how to work with people. Your first job builds your work ethic and teaches you professional habits early that will form your foundation later on.

Tip: Apps like Nextdoor and local WhatsApp groups are gold mines for neighborhood gigs. Do you have a neighbor with a new puppy and a hectic schedule? Congratulations, you just found your first hustle. If you're under eighteen, keep in mind that—depending on your state—you may need a work permit for certain jobs. A quick search online can tell you how to get one.

Networking Isn't Just for Businesspeople

You've probably heard the word "networking" tossed around, but here's a secret: It's not just for businesspeople with fancy job titles. Networking is something you can, and should, start building early. Whether you're in high school or college, the relationships you form now can help you when it's time to pursue your first job or internship.

Think of it this way: All those hours you spent trying to grow your Snapchat network, expand your Instagram following, and figure out who's hosting the next big party? That's networking! Now, we're not saying you need to bring your Instagram hustle straight into the job market; however, the skills you've developed in socializing, making connections, and keeping up with different platforms will translate into networking for your career. When you're ready to start looking for jobs, LinkedIn will replace your Snapchat, but it's the same concept. Start treating your social network like your future professional network. It'll pay off!

You Need Money, and You Need Experience. Let's Go!

When you enter your teens, you're going to want your independence. That often starts with the need to make your own money. You may want to join your friends at the mall, go to the movies on a Friday night, or save up for your first car. Whatever the case may be, the need for cash is a real motivator. We call it the Money Motivator, and it's the driving force behind why most young adults start thinking about getting a job.

The good news is, every job you take now—whether it's walking your neighbor's dog or working at your local skate shop—is a chance to learn skills that will make your future job search easier. Your first job likely won't be your end game, but it doesn't matter. Working at your local café or even reselling your old clothing online teaches you some transferable skills. No matter the job, you'll start building core skills like communication, time management, responsibility, and dealing with others. These are the same skills that'll carry you through subsequent roles and look impressive on your first résumé.

Elle Woods and The Ice-Cream Scooper

Lori:

"I could never do math. My brain just doesn't work like that, so I knew early on that I was never going to be an accountant. I always had the bug to get involved and work, but my parents wouldn't let me, which is what I really wanted to do."

Rachel:

"Oh yeah. In theory, babysitting seemed like a fun job where you could just play make-believe in someone else's home. Then, at a sleepover party, I had the pleasure of watching *When a Stranger Calls* and was too terrified to stay home alone for many years. So babysitting was out the door pretty quickly for me."

Lori:

As a teenager, I was very similar to how I am today. I was the overachiever as a student. I joined just about every club in high school that was offered. Yearbook committee, newspaper, the tennis team… I really did anything I could sink my teeth into and be involved. I was basically Elle Woods, minus the pink outfits and law degree. I was out there volunteering at a soup kitchen every Wednesday and reading books to kids at the public school next door. These weren't paying jobs, but I was desperate to be independent and find my path early on. I was all about trying to save the world one club at a time. My hustle was my extracurriculars."

Rachel:

"I love that you were such a joiner and trying to save the world. I was quite the opposite. I was out there just trying to save enough money for gas so I could drive to parties. I liked to work to have my freedom. One of my very first jobs in high school was working at a famous ice-cream shop one town over. I felt so cool in my tie-dyed T-shirts, and gave free ice cream to all my friends who would visit me. I remember being so excited when I was promoted to key holder, which felt very powerful as a teenager. I would close the shop early, pick up my friends, and roll into a party with a dozen pints of ice cream. Let's just say, I wasn't employee of the year…but I had cash, gas, and fun, so I reached my goals."

Lori:

"So you're saying we haven't changed? You were curating your social circle, and I was hustling, trying to find the edge!"

Start Strong: How Getting Involved Shapes Your Résumé

If you're not yet in the workforce, there are still plenty of ways to start building your résumé without a paycheck. Look around your school and community and start researching what clubs or extracurricular activities are offered. Finding opportunities to volunteer is another great thing to consider. You're not just filling up your schedule—you're learning valuable skills, from teamwork to project management. These experiences are all building blocks for your résumé, and they can start now.

Getting involved in meaningful activities not only helps you build experience—it helps you start networking. Whether you're applying for internships, jobs, or offering your time as a volunteer, club leaders, teachers, and mentors can offer advice and connections that will help you later.

Even "Boring" Jobs Will Teach You Something

We get it…you're probably not stoked about your first job. It may feel boring or repetitive. It may feel like you're not being used to your full capacity, and in most cases, you aren't yet. And that's okay. Remember, every job—no matter how basic—is a learning opportunity. Working at a local store? You're learning organization and responsibility. Babysitting your neighbor's kids? That's all about time management, patience, and communication. Take pride in whatever it is you commit to, and know that you're helping your future self.

Don't just go through the motions. Take every opportunity to learn how businesses operate, how projects are managed, and how people communicate. Even small tasks teach you something valuable that you'll use in your career down the line. The point here is to make the most of every opportunity, no matter how small it seems.

Creative Hustles = Experience That Counts

Maybe you don't have a traditional job right now, and that's just as good. You can get creative and create your own opportunities. Whether it's making handmade crafts and selling them on Etsy, or tutoring kids in your community, you're still gaining experience and building a portfolio. All this counts and you're essentially running your own "business," which teaches you different—yet just as valuable—skills. You're becoming a budding entrepreneur, and you may not even notice, but you are likely sharpening your skills in marketing, customer service, time management, and even finance. Plus, whenever you start creating your first résumé, those experiences can be highlighted and will help you stand out.

Crafting a Résumé and Building a Foundation

So, all this talk about your first job, joining clubs, and volunteering is leading us to this: your first résumé. It's okay if your first résumé looks simple—just think of it as your foundation. Once you have your foundation, everything you do down the line will be built on top of that. These are the building blocks for your future career. When you're ready to apply for a bigger role, you'll have a well-rounded résumé to back you up. Keep in mind that your first job or internship isn't the end goal—it's just step one in the process of building your career.

To Do Today

1. Make a list of any jobs (big or small, paid or unpaid) that you've held. Don't forget to add in volunteer work and any clubs or organizations to which you've offered your time.
2. Add specific skills you've gained from all your various activities.

From Mentors to References

Mentors are a great asset for several reasons. A mentor is any experienced and trusted person who can offer wisdom and perspectives that help you make informed decisions and overcome challenges, ultimately guiding you toward success in both your personal and professional life. They can help you build confidence and support you as you navigate this next chapter in your life.

This relationship can be formal—like a teacher, boss, or coach—or informal, such as a family friend or community leader. A mentor not only supports you in your growth, but becomes a trusted reference in your future job searches. They should able to speak firsthand about your work ethic, time management skills, overall personality, and goals. By cultivating these relationships early on, you create a network of support that can either help open doors to opportunities or simply offer a valuable reference when it's time to apply for your next position.

- Build upon that list from above and think about who you formed a relationship with in those jobs. Generate a mentor list of anyone you have connected with in any of those jobs. This should be someone you are comfortable contacting and asking if they would be comfortable being on your reference list. It's very important to ask before adding them, so they aren't caught off guard when called upon. We have seen this play out too many times—job seekers will add someone from a previous job without asking, and they either don't respond or don't give a glowing review. It's not worth adding someone on your reference list unless you know it's a slam dunk and they will sing your praises.

Five Takeaways to Planting the Seedlings

1. **Start Building Your Network Now:** Start connecting with people in your community who can help you in your future career search.
2. **Take on Jobs, Join Clubs, and/or Volunteer:** Every job, no matter how small, teaches you valuable lessons.
3. **Look for Every Learning Opportunity:** Even boring tasks can teach you something useful.
4. **Experiences are the Best Teachers:** They allow you to learn what you like and what you don't like. Take it all

in and start to understand where you enjoy spending your time.

5. **Find Mentors to Help Guide You:** They can offer advice, help with introductions, and ultimately become your references.

CHAPTER 2

WHERE TO HARVEST YOUR DREAM JOB

Right now, you might be staring down the finish line of school, stepping away from a job you've outgrown, or simply itching for a fresh start. Maybe you're a recent graduate feeling a mix of excitement and panic, wondering what comes after all those late-night study sessions and internships. Or maybe you've been in the workforce a few years, realized this path isn't quite the right fit, and are ready to pivot. Wherever you are, one big question lingers: *"What's next?"*

This chapter is your map to navigating the noisy, overwhelming, and confusing world of job hunting. We're not just going to talk about where to look; we're going to help you figure out what you're looking for and why it matters.

Step 1: Know What You're Growing

Before you start to harvest anything, you really need to know exactly what it is that you're planting. Take a moment and try to picture your job search like a farm. Are you going for a quick win, like grapes, with a fast-paced job with short learning curves? Or do you favor slow growing oak trees, which are more like long-term roles that lead to deep expertise and growth? Before you start applying, think hard about what you're intending to harvest.

Ask yourself:

- What industries excite me?
- Do I thrive in fast-paced environments or slower, more structured ones?
- What are my nonnegotiables (such as salary, mission, work-life balance, and distance from home)?
- What skills do I already have, and what skills do I want to develop?

The clearer you are on what you want, the easier it will be to spot the right opportunities and say no to the wrong ones.

Finding Jobs Before Wi-Fi

Lori:

"When I was in college, we practically had to send smoke signals to get a job. It's true! You'd sit there circling ads in the back of an actual newspaper. I used *The Hollywood Reporter* back then. We had no LinkedIn, no Indeed, no job boards.... No Wi-Fi for that matter. You picked up the landline, called a number, and prayed someone answered. Half the time you were leaving a voicemail on one of those giant answering machines, or faxing a résumé to a random office."

Rachel:

"Same here. My first job came through my cousin's friend who knew a guy who knew a guy...you get the picture. I ended up getting an interview at Laundry by Shelli Segal. And yes, we used to circle job ads in the newspaper like we were studying for a final. It sounds prehistoric now, but I remember actually going to a store in my town and picking out the perfect red marker for all my circling needs."

Lori:

"And speaking about using relationships...my first job as a production assistant was through my friend's mom. She heard about the job and made the intro. No online applications. No fancy portals. Just a good old referral network."

Rachel:

"Exactly. And while it's technically easier now to access job postings—with one click you're looking at fifty listings—the real challenge is standing out. Back then, fewer people even knew about a job unless they had the right newspaper or contact. Now? Everyone sees everything *instantly*."

Lori:

"Standing out is crucial. I actually stood out by becoming the butt of a joke, on air, during comedian Paula Poundstone's first TV show. They mocked the way I answered the phone, saying I sounded like I was trapped in a cage and couldn't believe someone had actually called. 'Are you okay?' they joked. 'Do you want to be rescued?' It was hilarious…and honestly? A great lesson in bringing a little more energy to the job, even when all you're doing is picking up the phone."

Rachel:

"Note to all college students: Answer the phone like you're absolutely thrilled to be alive."

Lori:

"Exactly! But seriously, it all goes back to this: Relationships, attitude, and hustle will always beat fancy apps. That's one thing that hasn't changed."

Rachel:

"Times have changed. Tools have changed. But making an impression on paper, online, or on the phone, is still everything."

Step 2: Look Where the Good Stuff Grows

Here's where most people mess up: They only look at major job boards like Indeed, LinkedIn, or Handshake. Those are important tools, but they're just the tip of the iceberg. The truth is some of the best opportunities are never posted publicly. They're shared in Slack channels, whispered in office kitchens, or casually mentioned over coffee.

Here are additional places to look for work:

1. Campus Career Center

It sounds basic, but most schools offer invaluable resources you're probably underusing like career coaches, résumé workshops, mock interviews, and direct employer connections. These offices often have exclusive job listings from alumni or companies that trust your school.

If you're in college, walk (no, *run*) into your career center freshman year. The staff there are paid to help you, but take it upon yourself to create strong bonds and relationships with the counselors who work in the career center. Remember that relationships are built over time, not the week before you graduate.

Set a reminder in your calendar to do a monthly in-person check-in at the career center. Be sure to introduce yourself to everyone who works there and ask the counselors their names and remember them. We recommend adding their contacts to your phone and refreshing your memory before walking in each time. Ask questions and deepen these relationships. Send a thoughtful follow-up thank-you note for their time, or a funny article about something you chatted about. You could even show up with a box of donuts to make a more impactful impression. Whatever it is, just make yourself memorable. Connections are key here, and visiting the career center is a great opportunity to strengthen them and increase your chances of being remembered when opportunities pop up.

2. Professors and TAs

Believe it or not, professors and teacher assistants (TAs) usually have deep networks in their fields. If you're in a communications program, your professor might know a PR firm hiring an intern. If you're in computer science, they might have tech company contacts. Ask them for leads; you'll be surprised how eager they are to help. A quick coffee chat could turn into a future job lead, mentorship, or priceless advice. If you can, offer to stay after class to help them collect papers or bring books to their car. Any chance you get to spend a little extra one-on-one time with your professor or TA will help you stand out from the crowd (who typically rush out of class as soon as they hear the bell).

3. Alumni Networks

Your school's alumni network is an untapped gold mine. Most alumni love to help current students because they see a little bit of themselves in you. Remember, these are people who've been exactly where you are, navigated the same campus, survived finals week, and launched their careers from the same starting point. Because of that shared experience, alumni are often more willing to offer advice, open doors, or even recommend you for jobs.

Whether they're working in industries that interest you, or hold positions at companies you admire, alumni can provide insider knowledge and referrals that can fast-track your job search. Reaching out through LinkedIn or your school's alumni database might feel intimidating, but most alumni genuinely want to help—especially when you show up with genuine enthusiasm, curiosity, and gratitude. Reach out to see if they would be willing to set up an informational interview where you can chat, pick their brains, and ask them for advice. Who doesn't want to talk about themselves and be admired?

4. Internships

These roles are foot-in-the-door opportunities, so don't sleep on them.

Interning in college is one of the most strategic ways to lay a solid foundation for your future job search. Think of internships as the building blocks of your career. They give you real-world experience, help you develop practical skills, and allow you to test-drive different industries or roles before committing to a full-time path. Even if the internship isn't in your dream career path, you're gaining insight into how teams work, what professional expectations look like, and how to manage your time and responsibilities in a real-world setting. That kind of experience not only makes your résumé stronger but gives you stories and examples to use in interviews, which helps you stand out from other new grads.

Beyond acquiring skills and experience, internships are one of the most effective ways to grow your professional network. Many students land their first full-time job through relationships built during an internship. Hiring managers often prefer to bring on people they already know and trust, so if you intern somewhere and make a great impression, you're already ahead of the game. Even if that company doesn't hire you, the people you meet there can connect you to future opportunities, write you references, or mentor you throughout your early career. Pursuing internships is like investing in a long-term career savings account: the earlier you start, the more it pays off.

Schedule Smart

At the beginning of each semester, keep the idea of an internship or part-time job in the back of your mind. Try to pack your class schedule on the same days, if possible, to leave days open for an internship or part-time job.

This is something students don't typically have in mind on day one, but if you craft your schedule right, you'll have time for all your classes and your work, which puts you ahead of the rest. Remember, even unpaid internships can pay huge dividends later through experience, references, and connections. Every internship you take is a building block toward your ultimate career.

You're not just fetching coffee—you're building skills, learning industries, and stacking your résumé.

5. Industry-Specific Job Boards

Industry-specific job boards can be a game-changer in your job search because they connect you directly with employers who are looking for candidates with your specific interests and skills. Unlike general job sites, these boards are curated for a particular field; whether it's fashion, tech, media, nonprofits, or entertainment, the listings tend to be more targeted, relevant, and current. Applying through these platforms means you're competing with a more focused group of applicants, not a random pool of thousands. Applying for jobs posted on industry-specific job boards gives you a better shot at standing out.

Even if you don't land a job right away, regularly browsing these boards helps you learn the language of the industry, spot trends in job titles or requirements, and understand what employers are really looking for. Over time, that knowledge helps you tailor your résumé, build the right skills, and apply with confidence when the right opportunity appears. It's not just about landing a job today—it's about staying plugged in so you're ready when the right job comes along.

6. Social Media and Newsletters

Following the right social media accounts and newsletters keeps you connected to the pulse of your industry, which is a huge advantage when you're job hunting. Many companies and recruiters share job openings on platforms like LinkedIn, Instagram, or X before they ever hit a job board. Some even post insider tips or hiring announcements exclusively to their followers. By staying active and engaged, you can be among the first to know about new roles, upcoming events, or networking opportunities.

Newsletters, especially ones focused on your field, curate relevant job postings, career advice, and industry news into one easy-to-digest format. Subscribing to just a few can help you stay informed without getting overwhelmed. Over time, this awareness gives you an edge: You'll be better prepared for interviews, more confident in conversations, and more likely to catch openings that perfectly match your goals. In short, staying plugged in keeps you top of mind, top of game, and ready when opportunity knocks.

7. Agencies: Your New Best Friends

If you know the industry you want to work in, find out what staffing agencies specialize in that field. Although we are a bit biased, we hear Grapevine is pretty fantastic for entertainment jobs.

Staffing agencies are like your job-search sidekicks. They connect you with companies you might never find on your own. What's more exciting than working with an agency? Working with multiple agencies at once. Often, they each have different client lists, so more agencies equals more opportunities. It's kind of like dating; we hate to say it, but it can be a number's game.

Make sure to always stay professional with agencies. This is a great way to test out your interview game. Be polite, extremely communicative, and always reliable. Think of your interaction with agencies as your scrimmage before the real game. Most agencies have created a file on you and are taking notes on your conversations so they can remember you.

You want to stand out and impress them, so always be on your A game. If they have a job that is a great match for you and they decide to send you out on it, remember: You are a reflection of them, so always put your best foot forward and make them look good. Even if that job doesn't work out, they will remember what a professional candidate you were and will be more likely to send you out again!

Five Takeaways to Harvest Your Dream Job

1. **Network Like It's a Dinner Party:** Build relationships with professors, TAs, alumni, and career counselors. These connections are key to unlocking job opportunities.
2. **Intern Like It's Your Job:** Internships are your training ground. Say yes, stay proactive, and treat every task as a chance to grow your résumé.
3. **Maximize Your Campus Resources:** Career centers, professors, and alumni networks are your hidden gems for job leads and guidance.
4. **Think Beyond Job Boards:** Industry-specific boards and newsletters often feature opportunities you won't find on typical job sites.
5. **Stay Plugged In:** Follow industry leaders and brands of interest on social media.

CHAPTER 3

CULTIVATING CONNECTIONS FOR SUCCESS

Networking isn't just about handing out business cards at a stuffy conference or adding strangers on LinkedIn. It's about building deeper relationships that will support and propel you throughout your career. We always tell our candidates that networking starts much earlier than you think; it's like searching for the right roommate or participating in a campus sorority or fraternity. At first, it may seem awkward or forced, but over time, you'll see that it's one of the most powerful tools you'll have for success.

The Foundation of Networking: Early Connections Matter

Networking begins long before you step into your first job. You've likely been networking since high school, whether you realized it or not. Those school clubs, group projects, and community service hours were your first opportunities to grow connections. Think about the peers, mentors, and teachers you met along the way who shaped your journey to this point.

In college, networking becomes even more crucial. The connections you make here aren't just future job leads—they're valuable sources of insight, advice, and mentorship. It takes time and effort to cultivate these relationships, but it's worth every ounce of energy. Networking isn't a one-time event; it's a long-term investment in your career.

The Power of Peer-to-Peer Connections

At first glance, peer networking might seem less rewarding than connecting with CEOs or senior executives. But peer-to-peer connections are often your strongest asset. Your college friends, classmates, and group project teammates are likely to become your future colleagues, co-founders, and even hiring managers. They're also navigating the same job market and career challenges, so they understand your perspective better than anyone.

Plus, peers often have access to opportunities and insights you might not find elsewhere. Don't underestimate the power of a simple coffee chat or a late-night study session where you swap job-hunting hacks and career advice. These small moments often lead to bigger things, and nurturing these relationships is just as important as impressing higher-ups.

Flashback: Networking in the Late '90s

Rachel:

When I was at Creative Artists Agency in the late '90s, assistant hangs were a whole thing. They weren't your carefully curated networking mixers of today but wild, late-night meet-ups that blurred the line between social and professional. There were no smartphones, no social media, no Monday morning blackmail photos. Just word of mouth, some questionable choices, and an unspoken bond that those nights created a network as strong as any LinkedIn connection you could make today. Once you walked out of the office on Friday, you were off the clock—really off. My fellow assistants and I would set a time and place before leaving work, and word would just spread. By 10:00 p.m., whatever venue was chosen for that particular night had wall-to-wall assistants. Think peak *Swingers*-era LA—unmarked bars behind velvet ropes, the all-night diners, the hustle by day and the party by night. Work hard, play harder. We bonded, we had fun, and most importantly, we were free.

Lori:

"In the '90s, networking was second nature. We didn't even call it that—it was just what we did. The film business was this exciting, mysterious beast, and I was obsessed. My friends and I would talk nonstop about scripts, who was repping what, and who was about to break out. We kept lists, we swapped hot tips, and we met up constantly at bars, readings, even random parties we heard about through someone's roommate. And forget Google Maps—we were flipping through The Thomas Guide, which was a huge book literally filled with maps of all the neighborhoods in LA. It was scrappy, chaotic, and so much fun."

Rachel:

"There was something about those pre-iPhone years that made it all feel looser, yet more connected. You couldn't just ghost someone…if you said you'd be there, you had to show up. And you did, because those connections mattered. We were all in the trenches together, trying to hustle our way up."

Lori:

"Exactly. The people I met in those early days? Still some of my closest friends. We were assistants, development girls, junior execs, agents-in-training, and now? Many of them are running the town. It all started over a shared love of movies and a night out that went way too late."

Standing Out to Build Your Network

Once you do begin to work, you'll need to keep up these connections and continue to make more. You can't expect to grow your network if you blend into the background. So whether you're an intern grabbing coffee or a new hire in your first "real" job, make it a priority to engage with colleagues, be proactive, and offer value wherever you can. People notice effort, positivity, and dedication. When you go the extra mile, you don't just impress your boss—you open the door to new connections.

Also, remember: Your boss's network can become your network, so look around. Don't hesitate to ask for introductions to people within their circle. Whether it's a quick and casual informational meeting with someone at the company or a lunch with a colleague from another department, these connections can help accelerate your career in ways you never imagined.

Conventional Networking Opportunities

If you want to get serious about building your professional network, here are some key places to focus your energy:

1. **Industry Conferences:** These are a gold mine for meeting professionals in your desired field and learning from thought leaders.
2. **Career Fairs:** A must for discovering internships and entry-level opportunities.
3. **Alumni Networking Events:** Connecting with alumni gives you access to insider knowledge and career advice from people who have been where you are.
4. **Trade Shows:** Great for connecting with people in your specific industry and learning about the latest trends.
5. **Sorority/Fraternity Events:** A built-in network of people who've already learned how to connect, collaborate, and support each other.
6. **Volunteer Opportunities:** Giving back builds your network while showcasing your skills and work ethic.
7. **LinkedIn:** A powerful tool for making connections with people who can help you find your dream job.
8. **Public Speaking Events:** Attend or participate in speaking events for a chance to meet other movers and shakers in your desired industry.
9. **Professional Development Classes:** Meet like-minded individuals while developing your skills.

Unconventional Networking Opportunities

Networking doesn't always have to be about formal events or industry mixers. Sometimes, the best networking happens in the most unexpected places, and can be just as fruitful as any formal event:

1. **Cultural Events:** Museums, concerts, and festivals can be the perfect setting for casual, meaningful conversations.
2. **Coffee Shops:** You'd be surprised how many professionals you can meet while waiting for your latte.
3. **Charity Events:** Show up where people rally for a good cause. There's real power in being in a room full of like-minded people who care about something bigger than themselves.
4. **Fitness Classes/Gym:** Health and wellness spaces are full of people with diverse interests and backgrounds. You never know who you'll meet on the treadmill.
5. **Art Galleries:** These venues are known for attracting creative professionals, providing a great opportunity to build connections in the art and design industries particularly.
6. **Sporting Events:** Whether it's a local game or a major league event, you'll find plenty of professionals bonding over their shared love of sports.
7. **Salons:** Believe it or not, conversations at the hair or nail salon can lead to valuable connections.
8. **Airports/Flights:** Travelers, especially frequent flyers, often make great networking connections because they're used to meeting new people in new places.

9. **Happy Hours:** Casual and relaxed, happy hours are a perfect way to connect with industry professionals outside of a formal setting.

Networking Is About Nurturing Relationships, Not Just Collecting Contacts

Networking isn't a checklist; it's an ongoing practice that requires nurturing, authenticity, and effort. Whether you're connecting with peers, professors, or executives, your goal is to build real, meaningful relationships that will support your growth long after you've landed your first job. Remember, it's not just about what you know, but who you know—and more importantly, who knows you.

Mentorship: Your Secret Career Weapon

While peer connections are vital, mentorship is the secret sauce that truly accelerates your career. Having a mentor who can guide you through the rough patches, introduce you to their network, and offer valuable feedback is priceless. A good mentor doesn't just give advice—they advocate for you when you're not in the room.

Reaching out to higher-ups within your desired industry or company can be intimidating, but it's a crucial step in expanding your network. Don't be afraid to ask for guidance or introductions. Mentors are often eager to share their knowledge and open doors for people they believe in.

Five Takeaways for Cultivating Connections for Success

1. **Start Early:** Networking begins in high school and continues throughout college and beyond. The sooner you start building relationships, the stronger your network will be.
2. **Peer Connections Matter:** Your classmates, roommates, and group project partners are future colleagues and valuable sources of insight and opportunities.
3. **Find a Mentor:** Seek out experienced professionals who can guide you. Mentorship is a powerful tool for career growth and potential connections.
4. **Stand Out in Your Job:** Whether you're an intern or a new hire, go above and beyond to make a positive impression. Your effort will lead to more connections and career advancement.
5. **Network Everywhere:** Networking doesn't just happen at formal events. Casual settings like coffee shops, fitness classes, and happy hours can be just as effective for building meaningful relationships.

CHAPTER 4

CRUSHING THE APPLICATION PROCESS

You've got your networking down, you know what industries excite you, and you've polished your résumé to perfection (more on that in Chapter 6). Now it's time to tackle the application process and master the art of standing out in a sea of applicants. Whether you're applying for your first job or eyeing a new opportunity, acing the application process is crucial to getting your foot in the door because the competition is fierce.

Two Roads to Hollywood: Neither Paved

Lori:

"I graduated college with lofty ambitions to work in the film business. My dad, Zack Norman, was a character actor at the time and he had me writing script coverage back in high school. Film and TV were in my blood. But I had one big dream: to work at CNN, specifically on *Showbiz Today*. It was the daily entertainment news show I watched religiously, and I was completely convinced that's where I belonged. I graduated college in 1992 with a love for entertainment and storytelling but was still too green to know how to get my foot in the door. As a bit of a stalling tactic, I signed up to volunteer and ended up working on an army base (long story!), like my own version of *Private Benjamin*.

"After that, I was gifted the time to backpack for six months through Europe, Greece, Thailand, Nepal, and Indonesia. I was soaking up the world and figuring things out. But by the end of January 1993, I told myself it was time to reel it in and get back to reality. I think I knew deep down that once I started my career trajectory, I wouldn't slow down (and I was right, because I still haven't). As I was heading home from that trip, my last hurrah, I called a good friend and got incredibly lucky. By Monday, I had landed a PA job working for her mom at NBC. One of those 'right place, right time' moments. But those moments only matter if you show up and deliver. I did.

"That job led to another PA gig, where I met a woman who worked at CNN. I took a chance, asked if I could interview, and eventually got the job at *Showbiz Today*. A total dream come true for me!

"Not long after, I realized that while journalism had its appeal, it wasn't where my heart truly was. But that role opened doors. I networked like crazy and got the chance to work at the newly formed Turner Pictures under Amy Pascal, part of the Turner/CNN family. And from there? I just kept building one relationship at a time until I landed another dream job: working with Alec Baldwin."

Rachel:

"My career trajectory was totally opposite. I faked my way into Hollywood (and it totally worked!). When I first moved from New York to LA in 1999, I had no clue how the entertainment industry worked. I didn't know the difference between an agency and a studio, and I definitely didn't know what 'rolling calls' meant.

"I had just wrapped a three-month stint in fashion back in New York, where I was technically the receptionist/showroom manager. When I moved to LA, I decided to rebrand myself as the 'Executive Assistant to Five Fashion Executives.' (Because…why not?)

"I walked into one of the recruiting agencies at the time and completely winged it. I didn't have my own email address, didn't own a computer, and had just gotten my very first flip phone. Although this is not recommended, I somehow convinced the recruiter I was 'excellent on the computer' (despite having never touched Excel), and they sent me on an interview that same day, before testing my typing or software skills. Dodged a bullet there! They said, 'You can go back and test later,' which I fully intended to do…until I never did.

"The interview was at a place called Creative Artists Agency (CAA). I had no clue what that was. I just smiled, nodded, and confidently BS'd my way through a conversation with the head of HR, spinning tales of managing high-level fashion executives and handling 'high-volume phones.' (I mean, technically true if you count scheduling couriers and ordering lunch for the showroom.)

"She hired me on the spot to assist two junior agents. I left the building still unsure what CAA actually was, but I had a job.

And a year later, after paying my dues, I got promoted to the desk of a managing partner. Fake it 'til you make it? I lived it."

Step 1: Understand What You're Applying For

Before you dive into the flood of job applications, take a moment to reflect on what you really want.

Ask yourself the following questions to ensure you're applying to roles that truly suit your aspirations:

- Is this the right opportunity for my long-term career goals?
- Does the company's culture align with my values?
- Will this position help me grow both professionally and personally?

Step 2: Highlight Relevant Experience

You don't need ten years of experience to apply for your first job, but you do need to highlight the experience that is most relevant. Tailor your résumé and cover letter to the job description, emphasizing transferable skills you've gained through internships, volunteering, or side hustles. It's all about showing how your experience will help you succeed in this new role.

Step 3: Showcase Transferable Skills

Even if you've never held a specific job, you've likely acquired a range of skills that can apply to any role. Strong communication, problem-solving, leadership, and teamwork are universally valuable. Think about your strengths and how they relate to the role, then make sure they're accentuated in your application.

Step 4: Consider the Financials

While passion is important, so is practicality. Make sure you're comfortable with the compensation package, including salary, benefits, and work flexibility. Factor in your financial needs, lifestyle, and any long-term goals you have for growth and advancement.

Step 5: Look Beyond the Salary—Growth and Culture Matter

Money is important, but don't overlook other aspects of the job that will influence your long-term happiness. Does the job offer career growth opportunities? What's the company's work culture like? In a post-COVID world where mental health is valued, work-life balance is more important than ever. Make sure the environment supports both your professional and personal well-being.

Step 6: Tailor Your Application for Each Role

Every job is different, so don't use a one-size-fits-all approach when applying. Customize your résumé and cover letter for each role, making sure to highlight how your experience aligns with the job requirements. It shows that you've taken the time to research the company and truly care about the position.

Step 7: Be Patient and Persistent

The application process can take time, so don't get discouraged if you don't hear back right away. And don't stop applying until you officially accept a job. You have no idea how many times we've seen candidates pass on jobs thinking they secured one, only for it not to work out for one reason or another. Keep applying, keep networking, and keep honing your skills. Each application is a step toward landing the right opportunity.

If you're feeling stuck or discouraged, we like to tell our candidates to "keep swirling the energy around." It means, make a few moves to keep that energy moving. Send some emails, make some calls, or even go to a networking event and collect some emails to follow up with when you get home. Don't just sit still and expect things to come to you. Keep that energy swirling!

Below is a checklist we've developed to help you stay organized and intentional during your job search.

Application Prep Checklist

1. **Career Goals**
    - Define your three-to-five-year career goals.
    - Identify the industries or roles that excite you.
2. **Skills and Experience**
    - List your top five skills.
    - Highlight key achievements from past internships or jobs.
3. **Work-Life Balance**
    - Identify your nonnegotiables (such as flexibility or remote work).
    - Define your ideal work culture.

4. **Company Research**
    - Find three companies that align with your values and career goals.
5. **Personal Branding**
    - Update your LinkedIn and résumé, making sure they match.
    - Create a professional email signature.
6. **Networking**
    - Reach out to key people (professors, alumni, mentors) for advice or job leads.
7. **Application Strategy**
    - Set a goal to apply to five to ten jobs per week.
    - Track your applications and follow up.

Five Takeaways for Crushing the Application Process

Align with Your Goals: Before applying, ensure the job fits your long-term career trajectory, work-life balance, and cultural values. It's about finding a role that aligns with your personal and professional aspirations.

1. **Tailor Your Application:** Customize your résumé and cover letter for each job, focusing on relevant experience and transferable skills that directly align with the job description.
2. **Highlight Transferable Skills:** Showcase skills like communication, leadership, and problem-solving, even if they're not directly tied to the specific role. These are valuable in any position.

3. **Consider the Bigger Picture:** Don't just focus on salary. Consider growth opportunities, work-life balance, and company culture when evaluating job opportunities.
4. **Stay Persistent:** The application process can take time. Keep applying, stay patient, and continue building your network. Every application is progress toward your dream job.
5. **Align with Your Goals:** The right job is not just about getting hired, it's about moving closer to the life you want. Use every application as a checkpoint: does this role fit your vision for growth, balance, and purpose? If it doesn't, keep going. The best offer is the one that aligns with your goals, not just your résumé.

CHAPTER 5

CRAFTING AN EFFECTIVE COVER LETTER

Your cover letter is your professional introduction and first impression. Make it easy to read, fast to understand, and hard to forget. Keep the vibe positive, professional, and personalized. Hiring managers are humans (for the most part), so help them see *you* behind the paper.

A strong cover letter can set you apart in a sea of applicants. It's your moment to highlight what makes you a great fit, but be sure to do it fast. Unless something grabs their attention, most hiring managers spend under ten seconds scanning an application. Your job is to make those seconds count, to try to hook them so they stay a little longer.

Cover Letters Aren't Résumés in Disguise

Rachel:

"Let me tell you something that drives me absolutely nuts: a cover letter that's just a long, boring recap of the résumé. Literally just paragraph after paragraph of "As you'll see on my résumé, I interned at XYZ and then I worked at ABC, and then I did this, and then I did that..." It's like, yes, I see your résumé. It's literally right here. Why are you just narrating it to me like it's story time?

"I have read thousands of cover letters, and one of my biggest pet peeves is when someone wastes their shot at making a memorable first impression by turning their letter into a résumé remix no one asked for. Others sound like a Wikipedia entry written by a robot who loves bullet points. I'm not trying to be mean, but...*pass*.

"Here's the truth: you get *maybe* ten seconds of someone's attention. If you're lucky. Use those seconds wisely. Tell us something new. Give us a glimpse of who you are, not what you've already done that we can clearly see on your résumé. We want personality, passion, a spark...anything but a copy-paste of your LinkedIn profile."

Lori:

"When you're applying to a company with multiple openings, don't just say 'I'm applying for the Assistant job' and send a mysterious link. Those links often lead to a black hole or five different jobs. Make it crystal clear which role you want. Copy and paste the job description or state the exact title (such as 'EA to Producer in Hancock Park'). Help us help you. Please don't make recruiters or hiring managers play detective or they will lose interest quickly. And remember to always save your files under your full name. Keep everything clean and concise.

"If you don't meet the mandatory job requirements, be upfront about it in your cover letter. Many recruiters or employers won't reply if you're missing must-haves, especially now, when the market is so crowded. We love proactivity and hustle, so if you want to sneak in through the back door, chimney, or even a secret tunnel, go for it.

"Don't send us a novel. After twenty years of reviewing applications, long cover letters make my eyes glaze over; I start dreaming of coffee. Show us why we should pause, admire your writing chops, and believe your transferable skills can do the trick. Be honest; it shows you actually read the job description instead of just winging it."

Why a Cover Letter Still Matters

Even if a job description says a cover letter is optional, submitting one shows extra effort, professionalism, and interest. It's your chance to demonstrate your personality, writing ability, and how you align with the role beyond your résumé.

Keys to a Great Cover Letter

1. Keep It Short: Aim for one to two short paragraphs max. Less is more. Make every word count.
2. Customize Every Time: Tailor your letter for each job. Mirror keywords from the job description. Avoid generic templates. Show them you took the time.

3. Be Professional, Not Robotic: Tone matters. Don't be too stiff, but don't get too casual. Find a balanced, polished, confident, and respectful tone.
4. Make It Personal: If you can address your letter to a specific name, use it. "Dear Hiring Manager," is always better than "To Whom It May Concern." If you don't know the name, keeping it formal is okay.
5. Show, Don't Tell: Give one strong example of something you've done that connects to the role. Use action verbs. Show enthusiasm without going over the top.
6. Think about how you can solve their problems. What need do you fill?

Cover Letter Format Breakdown

Opening: Grab the reader's attention, state your interest in the position, and mention the specific job title.

Body (one short paragraph): Highlight one to two key skills or experiences relevant to the job. Mirror some language from the job description.

Closing: Reiterate your interest, invite them to reach out, and include your contact info (email, phone number, LinkedIn profile with clickable link, and portfolio/socials, if relevant).

Cover Letter Tips

- Always save your cover letter as: FirstName_LastName_CoverLetter.
- Include your neighborhood, not your full address (for example, "based in West Hollywood").

- *Never* include a photo, as this can unintentionally invite bias. Employers should be focused on your skills, not your looks.
- Don't use AI to write your letter; your voice matters. Instead, use it to check grammar.
- If the job posting says no cover letters, don't send one. If it says cover letters are optional, send it but make it brief; it shows initiative.
- Put your contact info at the top of your cover letter: email, phone number, and LinkedIn profile with clickable link.

Ten Things to Never Put in Your Cover Letter

1. **A Rehash of Your Résumé**

   Don't waste the space repeating everything that's already listed. Your cover letter should add value, not echo your résumé.
2. **"To Whom It May Concern"**

   It's an outdated and impersonal salutation. Take the time to address your cover to a real person, or at least "Dear Hiring Team."
3. **Your Entire Life Story**

   This isn't the time to start at birth. Stay focused on what matters for the job.
4. **Overly Formal Language**

   "We beg to submit this humble application" sounds like you're auditioning for a period drama. Be professional but natural.
5. **Generic Traits Without Proof**

   Saying you're a "team player" or "hard worker" means nothing unless you back it up with a real example.

6. **Negativity About Past Jobs or Employers**

   No matter how toxic your last job was, keep it positive or neutral. Anything else is a red flag.

7. **Typos or the Wrong Company Name**

   This is an instant deal-breaker. Proofread closely, and double-check that you're actually addressing the right company.

8. **Unsolicited Salary Expectations**

   Unless specifically requested, don't bring up compensation in your cover letter. It's way too soon.

9. **Cringe Buzzwords**

   Terms like "guru," "ninja," or "rockstar" can make you sound unserious. Keep it clean, classic, and credible.

10. **Apologizing for What You Lack**

    It's okay to point out where your experience doesn't line up perfectly, but don't apologize for it. Employers already know no candidate checks every single box. Instead, frame it with confidence: acknowledge the gap, then pivot to how your strengths, transferable skills, and ability to learn make you a strong fit. The key is honesty without apology.

The Cover Letter That Gets You the Interview

Lori Zuker Briller
Beverly Hills, CA
email address | phone number | LinkedIn

Dear Hiring Manager,

I'm reaching out to express my interest in the Executive/Personal Assistant role supporting an entertainment entrepreneur. I've spent the last three years juggling calendars, coordinating talent, managing events, and keeping things running smoothly behind the scenes, and honestly, I love this kind of work. My background includes a mix of executive support, personal publicity, and client relations, and I've always thrived in fast-paced, high-pressure environments.

I know how to stay three steps ahead, communicate clearly, and handle sensitive situations with care and discretion. I'm excited about the idea of working closely with someone creative and entrepreneurial. I bring strong instincts, a calm presence, and a true appreciation for the kind of trust this role requires. Thanks so much for considering me, I'd love the chance to connect.

Warmly,
Lori Zuker Briller

Five Takeaways for Crafting an Effective Cover Letter

1. **Tailor Every Time:** Customize your cover letter for each job using keywords from the job description.
2. **Short and Sweet Wins:** Stick to one to two concise paragraphs. Show your value fast; hiring managers skim, not study.
3. **Use Your Own Voice:** Let your personality shine through. Write it yourself. AI can check grammar, but don't let it speak for you.
4. **Keep It Professional, Not Stiff:** Find the tone sweet spot: polished, confident, and respectful, but never too casual or robotic.
5. **Contact Info Counts:** Always include your email, phone, clickable LinkedIn link, and neighborhood (never your full address—scary!). Make it easy to reach you.

CHAPTER 6

THE PERFECT BLEND—YOUR PROFESSIONAL BRAND AND A RÉSUMÉ THAT POPS!

Résumés are our happy place. We have reviewed thousands over the years and have seen it all. We are here to remind you that your résumé is more than a document, it's your brand on paper! In this chapter, we'll show you how to craft a résumé that stands out, reflects your professional identity, and gets noticed in under ten seconds.

Your Résumé = Your First Impression

You may be perfect for the role you're pursing, but so are hundreds of others. What makes an employer or hiring manager stop on your résumé? Attention to detail, clean formatting, and a clear professional story.

This document should showcase your experience, skills, and career direction. It needs to be tailored, polished, and updated regularly as you grow.

Professional Brand on Display

Your résumé should align with the professional image you're building. It should not present your life story—just the most relevant and impressive highlights.

To prepare for this process, think about:

- What are your core strengths?
- What are opportunities are you seeking?
- How do your past roles prepare you for what's next?

Above all, when it comes to résumé writing, stay lean and mean. Less fluff, more clarity.

"Résumé Regrets and Rookie Mistakes"

Rachel:

"Okay, I have a really embarrassing confession. Back in the day when I worked at CAA but was starting my job hunt, I made the most embarrassing résumé mistake. I spelled the company name wrong. I wrote 'Creative Artist Agency' instead of "Creative Artists Agency." No 's.' It was not my finest hour."

Lori:

"Ouch! While it was a total rookie move, I am sure it's somewhat relatable. I would've passed over your résumé on principle because, as you know, I'm obsessed with résumés. It's like my religion."

Rachel:

"I had that version floating around for weeks before someone caught it. It was the biggest job on my résumé, and I STILL got it wrong. I was mortified. It still makes me cringe when I think about how many hiring managers probably rolled their eyes at my résumé and passed it over for one little typo. I was luckily enough to have a friend call it out for me."

Lori:

"That's why you ALWAYS have someone else read it over. Fresh eyes catch the stuff your brain autocorrects. Also, another pet peeve is a résumé that runs on and on for pages like a Cheesecake Factory menu. It's so long that you get to a point where you are so overwhelmed you just kind of shut down and don't want any of it. Instead, just pick the top five things that are relevant to the job you are targeting."

Rachel:

"Yes! I appreciate that people want to show the full breadth of their experience, which is great...but if the job is for an assistant, and you're leading with your senior thesis on sustainable fashion startups and one line at the bottom says, 'some light scheduling,' you've lost the plot."

Lori:

"Exactly. Employers aren't psychic. If the job description says, 'calendar management, booking travel, inbox management,' your résumé better be screaming 'ADMIN SKILLS HERE!' right at the top."

Rachel:

"Say it louder for the people in the back!"

Lori:

"You may think you're leveling up by skipping the admin stuff, but really? You're just making them think the role is beneath you. Don't make them guess. Show them how you'll make their life easier."

Résumé formatting cheat sheet

- **Use third person:** No "I" statements.
- **Bullet points only:** No long paragraphs.
- **Consistent spacing:** A clean layout = a clean mind.
- **Reverse chronological order:** Most recent experience goes first.
- **Font size 10–12:** No one wants to squint.
- **Save as PDF:** With your full name in the file title.

Avoid colorful fonts, wild formatting, or overly designed templates (we're looking at you, Canva). Chic, traditional, and simple always wins.

What to Include

- **Full Name, Phone, Email, LinkedIn**
- **Location:** Just your neighborhood or city, no full address.
- **Summary** (optional): Use this only if you have a clear and aligned story to tell.
- **Experience:** Relevant roles with bullet points that highlight your impact.

- **Education:** Unless you went to an Ivy League school or it's highly essential, this goes at the bottom.
- **Skills:** Both technical/ hard (Excel, Canva, Google Suite) and abstract/soft (communication, time management).
- **Awards and Certifications:** If relevant to the role.

What NOT to Include

- Hobbies like hiking (they won't help you get hired).
- Interests that aren't tied to the role.
- High school activities (after your first few years post-grad you can drop them).
- Fancy colors or fonts.
- Spelling or grammar mistakes. Ever.

Hard Skills vs. Soft Skills: What to Add to Your Résumé

When it comes to your résumé, it's important to show off both your hard skills and soft skills. Let's break down the difference.

Hard skills are the technical and job-specific abilities you've gained through education, training, or hands-on experience. These are measurable and teachable things you can usually prove with a certificate, a degree, or a portfolio.

Soft skills, on the other hand, are your personal attributes and interpersonal abilities. These are what help you work well with others and succeed on a team, even if they're harder to quantify.

Examples of Hard Skills:

- Microsoft Office or Teams
- Slack
- Zoom
- Graphic Design
- Video Editing
- Excel
- QuickBooks
- Coding Languages
- Foreign Languages
- Financial Forecasting
- Final Cut Pro

Examples of Soft Skills:

- Strong Communication
- Team Player Mentality
- Problem-Solving
- Time Management
- Leadership
- Attention to Detail
- Discretion and Confidentiality
- Emotional Intelligence
- Multitasker
- Adaptability
- Proactive Mindset

Tip: Listing these skills at the bottom of your résumé is a great start, but not quite enough. Make sure to back them up with examples in the body of your résumé. For example: If you say you're a strong communicator, highlight a job where you led presentations or managed client interactions. If you mention video editing, reference a specific project or platform you used. Hiring managers want to see proof to back it up, not just a list.

Mind Your Social Media Footprint (It's Part of Your Résumé Now)

Welcome to the digital age. Like it or not, your future employers will Google you. This is why, for the last ten years, we have been saying everything is permanent. Hopefully you came out of school unscathed, and no one took a video of you doing a keg stand, but if so... Now is the time to clean it all up!

Before you start applying for internships and jobs, be sure to Google yourself to see what comes up. Hopefully not much. Also, make sure to clean up all your social media. You want to make sure your social media story matches your résumé story.

If you're majoring in communications, your feed should look like someone who gets branding, storytelling, and professionalism. If you're pursuing a corporate job in finance, make sure your LinkedIn doesn't look like you're aiming for a creative job at a production company. As we like to say, **consistency = credibility!**

You have no idea how many of our clients ask for social media handles during the interviewing process. They want to do a vibe check and make sure the candidate they're meeting is not only professional, but a cultural fit for their organization. If your socials are private, you may be asked to accept a request from someone on their team, just so they can take a quick peek. To relieve some stress during your interviewing era, try to be mindful of your social media presence before you begin your search. Otherwise, you'll spend the night before an interview scrubbing your socials instead of going over mock interview questions.

Ask yourself: Are my posts something a future boss would want to see? We've had many clients ask to see a candidate's socials right after the meeting, which leaves very little time to thoughtfully go through your profiles to make sure they're appropriate. Consider this: If you are applying for a nanny job, and you have images of yourself drinking wine, a future boss may be put off by this. They don't want to picture their wholesome nanny spending every day with their kids, getting drunk at a bar. We always tell people: Keep your brand consistent.

Tip: Use your social media to show off your skills! Post about your internship, projects you're proud of, or causes you care about professionally. Your socials are essentially your digital handshake, so make it strong, confident, and unforgettable. This is your reminder to create a LinkedIn profile if you haven't yet. It's free, it's powerful, and it's one of the first places employers will check.

Keep It Current

Your résumé should grow with you. Every new job, skill, or certification? Add it. Keep your résumé updated so you're ready when opportunity knocks—especially when you're not even looking. We always tell people: have a résumé ready at all times. You never want to scramble when your dream job finds you first.

And yes, we get it, updating your résumé while employed can feel a little sneaky—like a quiet act of rebellion. But it's not betrayal; it's empowerment. On those tough days at work, it's a reminder that you have options. Consider it your ticket out, tucked safely in your back pocket.

Five Takeaways for Your Professional Brand and Résumé

1. **Your Résumé Is Your First Impression and Your Brand:** Your résumé is a snapshot of your professional identity. Keep it clear, tailored, and polished to tell a compelling career story that makes employers stop and notice within seconds.
2. **Keep It Clean, Consistent, and Professional:** Use simple formatting, third person, bullet points, consistent spacing, reverse chronological order, and a readable font. Avoid flashy fonts, colors, or overly designed templates. Save as a PDF with your full name.
3. **Include What Matters—Skip the Fluff:** Focus on relevant experience, core skills (both hard and soft), and accomplishments that align with your career goals. Leave out unrelated hobbies, high school info, and anything that doesn't add to your professional story.
4. **Update Regularly and Stay Ready:** Your résumé should grow with you. Add new roles, skills, and certifications as you go, so you're always prepared for opportunities. Keeping your résumé current shows you know your worth and are proactive about your career.
5. **Your Online Presence Is Part of Your Résumé:** Google yourself and clean up your social media before applying. Your online profiles should support the professional

brand your résumé presents. Create and maintain a strong LinkedIn profile. Think of your social media as your digital handshake. Consistency builds credibility!

CHAPTER 7

TURNING SOUR GRAPES INTO SWEET SUCCESS

How to Reframe Rejection and Stay in the Game

Rejection is inevitable. No matter how qualified, polished, or passionate you are, sometimes the answer will be no. And sometimes that "no" won't come with an explanation. Rejection stings, but it doesn't mean you failed. It means you're in the game.

In many cases, what seems like a perfect match on paper may not align with what's happening behind the scenes. Companies have priorities you can't see from the outside. There are nuances in every hiring process, and some decisions are made before the job even posts. You just have to trust the process and have faith that you will get a response if you're right for the job.

The Modern Job Market Is FAST

The hiring process today moves at lightning speed. With Zoom interviews, quick turnarounds, and AI screening tools, you have to stay alert. Check your email daily. Respond quickly. Ghosting goes both ways, and you don't want to be the one holding things up.

Sometimes you're not even dealing with a person. We've all screamed into the void trying to get a real human at the pharmacy or the airline customer service line. Job hunting can feel the same. If you are able to interact with a real hiring manager, be grateful. That's a window to learn and get a foot in the door, even if *that* specific job isn't the one.

The Job Was Never Yours—And That's Okay

Here's a harsh truth: Many big companies are legally required to publicly post jobs even if they already plan to promote someone internally. It's about compliance and fairness within the organization, not about you. So even if you were the perfect candidate on paper, the odds may have been stacked from the start.

Internal hiring is often preferred to keep morale high. Always hiring externally can make employees feel like there's no growth potential, which leads to disengagement. So yes, rejection is frustrating. But it's also reality. Don't internalize it; recognize it for what it is and try not to take it personally. You can remind yourself with every no: "It's not me, it's you."

Navigating Rejection with Resilience

Rejection can feel personal, but it's not a statement about your worth. It's just one small step in a longer path. The truth is, resilience is your superpower.

Here's how we'd like you to reframe rejection:

- **Acknowledge it.** Be bummed. It's okay to feel the sting.
- **Reflect on it.** Was your cover letter clear? Did your résumé match the job description? Could you have tailored things more?
- **Get feedback.** If you can, ask the hiring manager: "Is there anything I could improve for future opportunities?" You might not always get a response, but when you do, that feedback is gold.
- **Detach from the outcome.** You might've built the job up in your mind as the one. But sometimes the rejection is redirection. That job wasn't meant for you, and something better may already be on its way.

Sliding Doors Moments

Rachel:

"After a few years at CAA, I was deep in the trenches, trying to figure out my next move. I knew being a talent agent wasn't the right path for me. The 24/7 lifestyle in a role like that is extremely demanding, and I knew it wouldn't fulfill me. I had my heart set on a casting job at Universal Studios. It felt like *the* one: creative, fast-paced, everything I thought I wanted. I was in the running for a few different jobs at the time, but casting was the dream. At the same time, I was up for a production assistant job at a small start-up. I stalled for a while, holding out for the casting job. To my disappointment, I didn't get it. I was gutted. I genuinely thought that job had my name on it. Instead, I decided to settle on the production assistant job...which turned out to be a total disaster.

"It was owned by two wealthy playboys who had no prior experience in entertainment. They hired a bunch of employees from reputable entertainment companies to appear well connected. I couldn't quite tell if they really wanted to make movies or just play producers at parties. It may have been both. Luckily for my mental health, it wasn't long before the company crashed and burned.

"All this to say, that rejection, followed by an unhealthy workplace experience, gave me the push I didn't know I needed. I started to think outside the box. To dream a little differently. To start what would eventually become Grapevine. If I had gotten the casting job, I may never have become a recruiter. That was my 'Sliding Doors' moment, and I'm grateful for the door that *didn't* open."

Lori:

"I had my own version of that. I was up for a job as Leonardo DiCaprio's assistant, and I really wanted it. I'd just come off working in a very similar role, so I knew I had the chops. The roles were practically identical! I really had my heart set on the job and I nailed the interview (or so I thought). I was sure it was mine, until it wasn't. When I found out I didn't get the job, I was crushed, and honestly, confused. At the time, it felt like a huge loss. But looking back, I realize that if I had landed it, I likely would have stayed on the production track I thought I was supposed to be on. That one rejection quietly rerouted my entire path and it ended up being the best thing that didn't happen to me. Sometimes the things you think you want most are actually detours in disguise. Trust the timing, even when it stings. Especially when it stings!"

Rachel:

"Speaking from experience, your rejection is your redirection!"

Turn Frustration into Fuel

Let rejection drive reflection:

- What can I learn from this experience?
- How can I grow from this experience?
- Who can I connect with from this experience?

Even if they passed on you for this job, always ask: "Can I keep your contact for future opportunities?" You never know what could come next or who they might know. Maybe you weren't a fit for that particular role, but perhaps there is another opening in the company that suits you better. Maybe the recruiter knows someone outside the company hiring a similar role that could be right for you. Keep networking throughout the whole process, because you really never do know where it may lead you.

Final Thoughts: You Are Still Worthy

Don't let rejection knock you off your path. Meditate. Go for a walk. Phone a friend. Cry it out. Do what you need to do to move forward. You are not defined by a single job interview, or even ten of them. It's a numbers game. Stay aligned with what you want and keep going, because sometimes…that no is just making space for the YES that's meant for you.

We like to tell our candidates: Give yourself twenty-four hours to feel it, stew in it, be mad, whatever you feel you need to do, and then…LET IT GO and keep moving forward! Motion = momentum, so don't let this derail you from your greater goal.

Trust the Process and Be Kind to Yourself

Remember the way you speak to yourself in these moments are really important. Change "I didn't get the role" to "That job wasn't meant for me," or even, "The universe has bigger plans for me." The story you tell yourself will change the way you feel about the situation, and therefore, change your attitude toward the outcome. Your self talk will always affect the vibe you are putting out into the world. Make sure you are kind to yourself and be patient. Your next job could be right around the corner (even though it might not feel like it), and you don't want to miss it by being too distracted with a rejection. We promise, you will find work. And when you do, it's a whole new kind of stress. Just be where you are right now and try to have faith it's all working for your greatest good. Easier said than done, we know.

Five Takeaways for Turning Sour Grapes into Sweet Success

1. **Rejection Is Not Personal:** Even perfect candidates get passed over. Many hiring decisions are influenced by unseen factors. Rejection is not a reflection of your worth.

2. **Some Jobs Were Never Really Available:** Companies often post roles publicly due to legal requirements, even if they already have an internal hire lined up. Frustrating? Yes. But you're better off knowing it's not always about you.
3. **Resilience Is Your Superpower:** Feel the disappointment, but don't stay stuck in it. Reflect, learn, improve, and then move on. Rejection is often redirection.
4. **Always Ask for Feedback (and Stay Connected):** If a real human replies, that's a win. Ask if they can share what you could've done better, or if they can keep your info for the future. It's an opportunity to grow, and to network.
5. **Stay Ready, Stay Positive, Stay in Motion:** The job market moves fast, so be prompt and proactive. Your next opportunity could be one email away. Keep going. You're still in the game.

CHAPTER 8

REFINING YOUR INTERVIEW PREP

Preparation is key to acing any interview. Discover how to research, practice, and present yourself confidently during job interviews.

You wouldn't walk into a final exam without studying, so don't show up to an interview unprepared. Interviews are your time to shine, and the best way to stand out isn't just having a great résumé—it's being ready. Prepare to talk about your experience, your goals, and the company you're hoping to join.

Prep Is the New Flex

Lori:

"Unfortunately when I was on the job hunt and trying to prep for my interviews, there was no internet. No LinkedIn. No company Instagram with inspirational quotes and team-building photos. You couldn't just Google a company and easily learn about their culture and mission statement. We were flying blind. If you wanted intel, you had to be scrappy. I'd dig through old articles, read the trades, and ask anyone I knew for information. That was my version of research."

Rachel:

"I walked into my CAA interview and didn't even know what CAA was. Which now sounds absolutely unhinged. But in my defense, they didn't even have a website and I didn't have a computer. I was so green, and really didn't even know what the industry trades were."

Lori:

"But now? There are zero excuses. Between LinkedIn, Google, TikTok, podcasts, Reddit threads, and every digital footprint imaginable, not doing your research screams 'I'm lazy and not that interested.' Harsh, but true."

Rachel:

"Exactly. If you show up clueless, it's a red flag. Just a big, waving 'Don't hire me' flag."

Lori:

"Moral of the story? Be curious. Be scrappy. And do the homework. Because the person next to you absolutely is."

Do Your Due Diligence

Before you step foot (or log into Zoom) for your interview, know your stuff. A high level of prep tells employers that you're thoughtful and serious about the opportunity.

- **Research the company** like you're writing a paper on it. What's their mission? Who are their clients? What's in the news about them?
- **Study the job description** line by line. Think about how your background fits what they're looking for and come up with examples that show you've previously done what they need.
- **Look up your interviewer** (LinkedIn is your friend). Knowing their title, past experience, or even something you have in common can help you build rapport.
- **Understand the bigger picture.** Why is this role open? Did someone leave? Is the team growing? It's not only fair to ask, it's smart. We ask every client we work with about the history of the role because the answer often reveals more than the job description. Knowing why a position is available can give you valuable insight into team dynamics, leadership, and expectations. It can also help you decide if the opportunity is truly right for you. Remember that you are interviewing them—just as much as they are interviewing you—to make sure it is a match.

Prepare to Talk About...You

This isn't the time to be humble or vague. In preparation for a job interview, be ready with:

- **Clear, specific examples** of times you solved a problem, improved a system, or added value in a previous job or internship.
- **Your "why"**—why this company, this industry, this role.

- **Your long-term goals** and how this job fits into the bigger picture.

Interview Etiquette and First Impressions

Whether in person or over Zoom, the basics still matter.

<u>For Zoom:</u>

- Find a quiet space with a clean background and good l ighting.
- Test your tech *before* the interview.
- Dress like it's in person, at least from the waist up!

<u>For In Person:</u>

- Arrive ten to fifteen minutes early, not thirty (that's awkward).
- Dress appropriately for the company culture (when in doubt, go a little more polished).
- Be kind and professional to *everyone*. You never know who's watching. (Seriously, the receptionist at the front desk might have the hiring manager's ear.)

Reference Reality Check

Before listing your references, make sure they're ready to go. Call or email your references in advance. Confirm that their contact info is current and that they're comfortable speaking on your behalf. Give them a heads-up about the role and what might come up so they can speak to your strengths. There is nothing worse than a hiring manager reaching out and getting ghosted—or worse, a lukewarm response.

Practice Makes Perfect

While you can't predict every question, some common ones show up again and again. These questions may come up in interviews, so use them to rehearse and refine your answers. You don't need to memorize anything, but you should be ready to speak clearly and confidently.

Practice Interview Questions

- Tell me about your employment history and why each role ended.
- Can you give me a detailed description of some of your responsibilities in your last role?
- Walk me through a typical day. How do you organize and prioritize your schedule?
- How do you feel about communication after work hours? Are you more of a nine-to-five employee, or will you respond to important calls and emails after hours or on weekends if necessary?
- Do you prefer working independently or as part of a team?
- Can you describe the type of environment or work culture in which you are most productive and happy?
- What are your strengths?
- What do you think you need to improve on? (Trick question—always do a positive spin.)
- How would you describe your personality under pressure?
- What are three adjectives that best describe you?
- Tell me about a situation where you had to fix a mistake or recover from a dropped ball. How did you handle it? What did you learn?

- Can you share an example of a project you worked on that you're most proud of?
- What software do you use regularly?

Tip: Practice answering these questions out loud—or better yet, record yourself. You'll be surprised how much more confident you sound the second (or third) time around. Remember, interviews aren't about being perfect. They are about being prepared. Do the work and be yourself. That combo is unstoppable.

Your Turn to Ask Some Questions

At the end of most interviews, the interviewer will ask if you have any questions for them. This is your golden opportunity to show your curiosity, emotional intelligence, and genuine interest in the job. Always be prepared with at least two or three thoughtful questions that you have rehearsed—but act natural, of course. A few great topics to ask them about are team culture, how success is measured, and what keeps their employees excited to show up.

This is also a moment where you can lose them if you ask the *wrong* questions. For instance, asking about salary or time off in the first interview—even if you're dying to know—is generally a bad move. Here's the logic:

- It shifts the focus too early from value to compensation.
- It can make you seem transactional—like you're more interested in the paycheck than the opportunity or the company's mission.
- It skips over the most important question: Are you even a good fit for the role?

The first interview isn't about what the company can do for you. It's about showing them what *you* can bring to the table.

Unhinged Interview Moments: A Cautionary Tale

Rachel:

"I have the craziest story. Like, truly unhinged. Taboo interview moments? This one lives at the top of the Hall of Shame.

"We've interviewed thousands of candidates over the past twenty years at Grapevine, and sometimes I feel like I'm stuck in a rom-com montage. You know the one where someone goes on ten first dates and every single person says something more ridiculous than the last?

"This was back in the early days of our company, before we had a proper office and well before Zoom ruled our lives. I was working out of my dining room and doing interviews at the Coffee Bean. Yep, *that* Coffee Bean—where I met Lori for the first time. It became our unofficial Grapevine HQ. Between the sound of ice blending and espresso orders being yelled over the counter, I'd snag a table outside.

"One day, I'm meeting a candidate who came highly referred by a friend. We sit down and she reaches into her bag. Naturally, I think she's pulling out a résumé. Nope. She pulls out a pack of cigarettes. Then, dead serious, she asks: 'Mind if I smoke?'

"I was so stunned I didn't even know how to process it. And instead of saying what I should have, which was 'I absolutely do mind,' I panicked and channeled awkward-chill-girl energy: 'Sure…yeah…totally cool…you do you.'

"And then—as if this wasn't enough—she lit up and blew smoke directly into my face as if we were two girlfriends at a

Paris café and not in the middle of a real job interview. I was done. *Immediately no.* Like, please-never-contact-us-again level no. So in case it has never been said to you explicitly: Please. Don't smoke at your job interview!"

Lori:

"That story lives rent-free in my head. I haven't had anything quite that cinematic happen, but the amount of bizarre, unprofessional behavior I've seen—especially from people who *really* want the job—is still staggering.

"There's this weird misconception that because we're the agency and not the direct employer, we somehow don't count. Let me clear that up real quick: We matter. A lot.

"As recruiters, we're your gatekeepers. Your first line of defense. If you blow it with us (or blow smoke in our faces), you don't make it to the next round. Period.

"Before COVID, when I used to do in-person meetings in my home office, I gave people incredibly detailed directions, like, 'the door is red, the chair is blue, park here not there' levels of detail. And still, people would knock on my neighbor's door. Others showed up late, dressed like they rolled out of bed, chewing gum and wearing ripped jeans. This was not brunch. This was supposed to be the first step toward a real job.

"And now, with Zoom? Oh, we've entered a whole new era of weird. I've had people walking their dog mid-interview, calling from the front seat of their car, Zooming in pajamas. One candidate was literally chatting with me while pacing around a grocery store. You cannot make this stuff up.

"Here's the deal when working with a recruiter. We're not just pitching you for one job…we're often advocating for you across multiple opportunities. So if you ghost us, delay responses, dress inappropriately, miss deadlines, or don't take the process seriously, you're out. That includes no-shows (yes, we've had people accept jobs and then…disappear). It's wild enough out here. Don't be the wild one."

What Not to Ask, and What to Ask Instead

Five Unapproved Questions to Avoid in Your First Interview

1. **"How much does this job pay?"**

   Talking salary too early can make you seem focused on compensation instead of contribution. Save it for later in the process.
2. **"What's your vacation policy?"**

   Asking about time off before you've even landed the job sends the wrong message. Focus on what you can bring to the role first.
3. **"How soon can I get promoted?"**

   This question can come off as impatient or entitled. Show interest in learning and excelling in this role first.
4. **"Do you do background checks or monitor social media?"**

   Even if you're asking innocently, this can raise red flags and make the interviewer question your professionalism.
5. **"Can I work from home whenever I want?"**

   Flexibility is important but asking about special accommodations before you're even hired can signal a lack of commitment. Learn the company culture first, then discuss options if necessary.

Five Approved Questions That Show You're Curious and Engaged

1. **"What are the top priorities for this role in the first few months?"**

   Shows you're already thinking about how to contribute and hit the ground running.
2. **"What does a typical day or week look like for someone in this position?"**

   Helps you visualize the role and demonstrates curiosity about how things really work day-to-day.
3. **"What qualities make someone successful on this team?"**

   Signals self-awareness, emotional intelligence, and a desire to align with the team's values and working style.
4. **"What's your favorite thing about working here?"**

   Softens the conversation and often leads to an honest, personal answer. It gives insight into company culture and reminds the interviewer that you're interviewing them just as much as they're interviewing you.
5. **"Can you tell me more about the person who held this role before and why they moved on?"**

   A smart, subtle way to gather information about the position's history, growth opportunities, or potential challenges, without sounding negative.

We like to tell people to always follow the interviewer's lead. If they ask you your salary expectations in the first round, answer honestly but briefly, and try to keep the conversation focused on how you fit the role.

If you're moving forward to a second interview or receiving an offer, *that's* the time to talk numbers, vacation, sick policy, and so on. By then, you've shown your value, and the negotiation becomes a mutual one. Remember: You will cross that bridge when you get there.

Interview Prep Checklist

1. **Research and Homework**
    - Look up the company's mission, values, recent news, socials, and leadership
    - Study the full job description, highlighting key responsibilities and qualifications
    - Search for your interviewer(s) on Google and LinkedIn
    - Learn why the role is open (growth? replacement?) if possible
    - Prepare two to three thoughtful questions to ask during the interview
2. **Know Your Talking Points**
    - Practice your "Tell me about yourself" answer
    - Have two to three solid examples of past accomplishments
    - Be ready to explain why you're interested in *this* company and *this* role
    - Know your strengths, and be prepared to share a weakness (with a positive spin)
    - Clarify your short- and long-term goals
3. **Set the Scene**
    - For Zoom: test lighting, camera angles, internet connection, and audio

- For Zoom: tidy your background and dress professionally from the waist up
- For in person: map the route and plan to arrive ten to fifteen minutes early
- For in person: dress slightly more polished than expected; however, never use excessive makeup or wear clunky jewelry that can be a distraction. Also stay away from perfume, as people may have an aversion to certain scents.
- Be polite and presentable to everyone you meet

4. **Reference Ready**
   - Confirm your references are reachable and prepared to speak on your behalf
   - Share job details with them so they can tailor their support
5. **Practice and Polish**
   - Rehearse common interview questions out loud
   - Record yourself speaking to catch pacing, tone, or filler words (try to eliminate ums and likes)
   - Prepare closing remarks (why you're excited and a thank you)
   - Send a thank-you email the same day

Five Takeaways for Refining Your Interview Prep

1. **Preparation Shows Professionalism:** Do your homework on the company, job description, and interviewer. It signals you're serious, capable, and thoughtful.

2. **Be Ready with Real Examples:** Interviewers want to hear specific, relevant stories that show how you solve problems, contribute to a team, and stay organized.
3. **First Impressions Matter:** Whether on Zoom or in person, how you present yourself—ideally on time, well-dressed, and courteous to everyone—sets the tone.
4. **Save Questions about Money and Perks:** Focus the first interview on value, fit, and curiosity. Asking about salary or time off too soon can be a turnoff.
5. **Ask Smart, Reflective Questions:** End the interview strong by asking thoughtful questions that show you've done your research and are invested in finding the right fit, not just a job.

CHAPTER 9

A TOAST OF GRATITUDE WITH THE PERFECT THANK-YOU NOTE AND FOLLOW-UP ETIQUETTE

Gratitude goes a long way in building relationships. Learn how to craft thoughtful thank-you notes and follow up professionally after an interview.

One of the most powerful tools in your job search arsenal is also one of the most frequently skipped: the thank-you note. Sending a thank-you note is a nonnegotiable. You might think your glowing personality and perfectly curated résumé speak for themselves—and maybe they do!—but a thoughtful follow-up can reinforce your strengths while demonstrating professionalism. In a competitive job market, the thank-you note will leave a lasting impression that sets you apart from other candidates. It isn't optional—it's strategy.

Why Thank-You Notes Matter

A thank-you note is more than just a polite gesture. It shows you're thoughtful and serious about the role. In a sea of applicants, the candidates who follow up professionally are often the ones who get remembered most, and sometimes, the one who gets the offer.

Hiring managers are paying attention to how you communicate during the interview process and beyond. Do you follow up? Are you articulate? Are you enthusiastic but not overbearing? It's all part of the test. Your thank-you note gives you one last opportunity to make your case.

If you want to really stand out and go the extra mile, write a handwritten note in addition to your email. Especially for industries or roles where relationships and personal touches matter. In our digital world, a handwritten thank-you can actually feel like a breath of fresh air. Treat every communication like it matters… because it does!

The Interview Isn't Over Until You Hit Send

Rachel:

"We advise our candidates to email their thank-you note within a couple hours of the interview."

Lori:

"Yes please! And now that everyone has pivoted to email notes, it's easier than ever. Although I still love a good old-fashioned handwritten thank-you note. I know those days are fading fast—like pen pals and landlines—but there was real effort involved: You picked out a card, found a stamp, looked up the address, and put pen to paper. It meant something. But I get that times have changed. I'm just happy as long as you send the note. This is why I am so adamant about reminding our candidates to do so. Whenever I send someone into a meeting, I double check that they have every possible tool to work with, including the client's name (double check spelling), meeting time, what to wear, and Zoom tips. I even say, 'After the call, please email me how it went and send a thank-you I can forward to the client.' And yet...about 50 percent don't do it. Or worse, they'll send me a text like: 'Hey Lori, can you let the client know I had a great time?' Huh? Pardon? That is *not* a thank-you note! And it's not just the younger candidates I'm speaking of.... I've seen seasoned professionals miss the mark completely. Your follow-up should be thoughtful, personalized, and directed to the person you met. Show appreciation. It's not rocket science, but it is a lost art.

"If you really want the job, prove it. Follow up. Say thank you. It might seem small, but it can be the difference between an offer and a rejection."

Rachel:

"We've seen it happen so many times. A candidate crushes the interview, the client likes them, there's interest...and then, radio silence. No thank-you note. No follow-up. Just...nothing. And guess what? That silence is often the dealbreaker.

"We recently had a huge celebrity client flat-out reject a candidate he genuinely liked because he never received a simple thank-you note. This candidate had gone through three rounds of interviews with the team and finally got to go to this actor's home for the final meeting. After an hour together, the meeting ended and both parties called to let us know it felt like a perfect match. As always, we had told the candidate to send a thank-you note directly after the meeting—but no note was sent. She must have been so excited about the possible job opportunity and perhaps thought that since it was already round four, maybe it wasn't as important to send a follow up. The day turned to night, and the note never came. By the next morning, it was too late. The client called first thing and told me he decided to pass on this candidate. He said, had it been based off personality and experience alone, she would have been a shoo-in. There was one other candidate in the running and 'what swung the decision was her lack of professionalism' by not sending a thank-you note for his time. As you can imagine, the candidate was shocked and heartbroken when I called to deliver the bad news. I explained that, from the client's perspective, it's a red flag. If you can't be bothered to follow up with a short note of appreciation, how can he trust you to represent his business? This was a major job, and he needed someone with excellent attention to detail and meticulous follow-through. Quite simply, she failed the test. I understood and kind of respected the client for having the foresight to know what he needed, and that he stuck to his boundary. It's job etiquette 101. And it's an easily avoidable mistake. Just. Send. The. Note."

What to Say, and What Not to Say

A great thank-you note is brief, thoughtful, and specific. It's not a recap of your résumé, nor is it the time to bring up salary, benefits, or anything that feels transactional. The tone should be warm and professional—not overly casual or robotic.

Do Include:

- Genuine appreciation for their time and the opportunity to meet. Try to make your thank-you note less generic so you stand out. Bonus points for not starting with, "Thank you so much for taking the time to meet with me today…" Snooze. Challenge yourself to start off with a more creative opener to stand out from the rest.
- A mention of something specific you discussed during the interview, such as: "So nice meeting a fellow New Yorker" or "Go Lakers! It was so much fun connecting on our mutual love for our favorite team." Just a detail or two to make them remember your connection.
- A reaffirmation of your interest in the position. This is your opportunity to show your enthusiasm, which everyone looking to make a hire wants. Don't waste it!
- A one-sentence reminder of why you're a strong fit. Include your top one or two skills, ideally ones you know they really need in their next hire.
- A professional sign-off with your full name and contact info. The hiring team may have really liked you but after a long day of interviews, perhaps your résumé is at the bottom of the pile. Set yourself up for success and make yourself easily accessible should they want to reach out again.

Don't Include:

- Typos, grammatical mistakes, or run-on sentences
- Desperation or "please hire me" energy
- Questions about salary, start dates, or next steps (unless prompted)

- A copy-paste template that doesn't feel personalized
- Emojis, slang, or overly casual language (you're not texting a friend)
- A text, DM, or LinkedIn message in place of a proper note

Subject: Thank You—Rachel Zaslansky Sheer

Dear Lori,

I really enjoyed our conversation today; it was such a fun surprise to connect over our shared love of documentary films. I left our meeting feeling energized and even more excited about the Assistant to Marketing Executive role at Amazon.

The way your team is leaning into digital strategy really stood out to me. With my background in content creation and campaign management, I'd love the chance to help bring that vision to life and support your next phase of growth.

Thank you again for the opportunity to speak. I truly appreciate your time and the insight you shared. Please don't hesitate to reach out if you need anything further. I'd be thrilled to continue the conversation.

Best regards,
Rachel Zaslansky Sheer
[Your Phone Number]
[Your Email Address]

Tips for Thank-You Emails

- **Proofread.** Then proofread again. Typos in a thank-you note are most likely a deal breaker because it automatically highlights your lack of detail.
- **Use their name—and spell it correctly.** Double-check if it's "Sarah" or "Sara." Details matter.
- **Skip the templates.** A thank-you note that sounds like it was written by AI in five seconds won't cut it and won't make you stand out.
- **Avoid over-following up.** If you haven't heard back after a week, it's okay to send one gentle nudge. After that, let it go unless they gave you a timeline or follow-up date.
- **Include each individual.** If you met more than one person in the meeting, be sure to send a personalized thank-you note to each one. Don't forget to collect all the names before you leave the meeting.

Five Takeaways for the Perfect Thank-You Note and Follow-Up Etiquette

1. **Send a Thank-You Note:** It's a professional courtesy. Plus, if you send a thank-you note within a few hours of the interview, it will set you apart.
2. **Make It Personal:** Reference something specific from the conversation to show genuine interest.
3. **Keep It Short and Sincere:** You're reinforcing the connection, not reapplying for the job.
4. **Be Polished and Error-Free:** Mistakes can undermine even the best message.
5. **Don't Overdo It:** One follow-up is great. Ten is a red flag.

CHAPTER 10

THE FINAL SWIRL—YOU GOT THE OFFER, BUT DO YOU WANT IT?

You've made it through interviews, thank-you notes, and probably some ghosting here and there. Finally, there it is: THE OFFER. That long-awaited email or phone call telling you you've been chosen. Make no mistake, being selected is a big deal. You outshined the competition, and your hard work paid off. But before you shout "YES!!!" take a breath. This is the moment most people rush through. You're so caught up in the chaos of job hunting (and wanting it to end) that you forget to pause and ask yourself the most important question:

Do I really want this job…or do I just want to be wanted?

This isn't about ego; it's about job alignment.

Job alignment is when a job matches up with who you are and where you want to go—not just in terms of skills, but values, goals, lifestyle, and energy. It's the "Does this feel right?" gut check, plus the logical checklist.

Job alignment is when these five things line up:

1. **Your Skills Match the Role**
   You're not constantly faking it or swimming upstream. The job plays to your strengths, with room to grow.
2. **The Work Feels Meaningful to You**
   You don't have to change the world, but you *should* care about the product, people, mission, or impact.
3. **The Culture and Pace Fit Your Personality**
   Are they Type A? Casual? Corporate? Fast and furious? You'll thrive in an environment that matches your energy—not drains it.
4. **The Compensation Supports Your Life**
   The salary, benefits, and flexibility allow you to live, not just survive.
5. **The Role Moves You Toward Your Bigger Goals**
   It doesn't have to be forever, but it should be a stepping stone—not a sidestep or a dead end.

When you're in job alignment, things click. You show up with energy. You grow. You feel chosen, not just employed. You are inspired and feel good. When you're out of alignment, you feel it fast. Stress. Dread. Sunday scaries on steroids.

That's why we push candidates to pause before saying yes. Because the right job doesn't just check boxes…it makes you feel like you belong there.

Before you accept, give yourself permission to check in. Does this opportunity match your values, goals, and energy? Will you be happy here, not just for the next six months but in the long run? The last thing you will want to do is restart your job search in six months, so let's avoid that now.

This chapter is about owning your worth, asking the right questions, and remembering that saying yes to a job is also saying yes to a version of your future. You deserve to get this part right. We are here to remind you that you're not just lucky to get an offer—you're valuable. Let's make sure you treat yourself that way.

Don't Talk Yourself Into a Job You'll Ghost

Lori:

"We see this all the time with candidates who are just so over the job search that they'll take literally anything. We've been there and we get it; the process can wear you down. You may be exhausted or financially unstable, or just desperate for the hunt to be over. But this moment is when some candidates do themselves a great disservice and start negotiating against themselves."

Rachel:

"We can usually tell when they start saying things like, 'Well…the salary's not what I hoped, but I'll make it work,' or 'I know it's not exactly what I want, but I need to just take something.'"

Lori:

"We've watched those same candidates burn out quickly. A week or two in, and they're texting us, 'Ugh, I think I made a mistake,' or ghosting the job entirely, which is a really bad look. Just last week a candidate totally ghosted a client of ours because she wasn't listening to her gut and was ignoring the red flags, only to wake up on what was supposed to be day one and go 'I don't want this job.'"

Rachel:

"Now, because you didn't speak up earlier, you may have burned a bridge. This is avoidable if you allow yourself to pause and reflect before accepting any offer. We encourage you to make sure you are in job alignment. We are not saying you must hold out forever for a unicorn dream job, but we *are* saying: Don't talk yourself into a job you know in your gut isn't the right fit."

Lori:

"It's time to be really honest with yourself. We're here to help you find a job that aligns, not one that burns you out and ends in a messy exit. There's nothing wrong with saying, 'You know what? I'm not sure this is the right fit.' Trust me, it will save you a lot of time and energy in the long run, even though it may not seem like it now."

Step 1: Evaluate the Offer—Beyond the Salary

Yes, the number matters. But a job offer is more than a paycheck. Ask yourself:

- **Benefits:** Are there health, dental, vision, 401(k), mental health support, and PTO? If so, how soon do they kick in? A lot of our clients offer benefits after ninety days.
- **Work-Life Balance:** Are you expected to be "on" 24/7, or do they respect boundaries?
- **Commute/Location:** Will this impact your quality of life? Will your commute be realistic, or will you burn out after the new job excitement wears off?

- **Growth Potential:** Is there a clear path to level up?
- **Company Culture:** Does it feel positive and supportive? Or like burnout central?
- **The New Team:** Do you want to work with these people every day?

A bigger paycheck doesn't always mean a better life, so these are important things to consider before you say yes.

Step 2: Ask Questions

Before accepting, it's okay (and expected) to ask for clarification. Consider questions such as:

- "Can you walk me through how performance reviews and raises work?"
- "What does onboarding look like in the first ninety days?"
- "How flexible is the remote/in-office schedule?"

If they get offended or annoyed by these questions at this stage of the process, that's a big red flag.

Step 3: Negotiate (Yes, You Can)

Most salary offers have some wiggle room. Even entry-level ones. You are more than welcome to research the average salary for this role in your city/industry. It doesn't mean a potential employer will give you what you want, but it doesn't hurt to ask if you feel strongly about it. If you do, be respectful, confident, and kind. They may not have it in the budget to go up and that's okay. You advocated for yourself, and hopefully—once you prove yourself after six to twelve months—you will be eligible for a raise.

Step 4: Know When to Walk Away

Sometimes the offer looks good on paper but doesn't feel right. Trust your gut, and walk away if:

- The vibe shifts the moment you ask questions.
- They pressure you to decide immediately.
- You find out the role isn't quite what they sold you.
- The salary is well below industry standard, and they won't negotiate.

You deserve a job that values you. You're not just filling a seat.

Step 5: Get It in Writing

Once you agree to terms, ask for everything in writing before giving notice anywhere else. In the document, look for:

- Salary and pay frequency
- Title
- Start date
- Benefits summary
- Any bonuses, stipends, or perks

Don't start a job based on a "verbal agreement." Protect yourself. You're a professional now.

Offer Evaluation Checklist

Use this to review any job offer before accepting. If you can't check most of these off, ask questions or think twice.

Responsibilities

- Do I clearly understand the day-to-day responsibilities?
- Does this align with my skills and long-term goals?

Compensation

- Is the base salary fair and aligned with market rate?
- Are there bonuses, equity, or signing incentives?

Benefits

- Health, dental, and vision coverage
- Retirement plan (401k, match?)
- Mental health or wellness programs
- Paid time off (vacation, sick days, and holidays)

Work-Life Balance

- Reasonable hours and expectations
- Flexibility in schedule or location (remote/hybrid/in-office)
- Clear policies on overtime and availability

Culture

- Do I like the team/manager?
- Did they seem respectful and aligned with my values?
- Is there room to grow?

Growth

- Is there a path to advance?
- Do they invest in training, mentorship, or continued learning?

The Bold Truth

- Never feel "greedy" for negotiating—feel empowered.
- Don't be afraid to ask for twenty-four to forty-eight hours to think it over.
- The best employers *expect* you to ask questions.
- A job is a two-way street. You're interviewing them too.

Five Takeaways for You Got the Offer, But Do You Want It?

1. **Maintain Confidence:** You're not lucky to get an offer—you earned it. Approach this moment from a place of confidence, not desperation.
2. **Evaluate the Full Picture:** Salary is just one piece of the puzzle. Take job alignment, culture, benefits, growth, and your own happiness into account.
3. **Negotiation Is Expected:** Done respectfully, negotiation shows professionalism and self-worth.
4. **Trust Your Gut:** If it feels off, pay attention. Sometimes walking away is the most powerful move.
5. **Put It in Writing:** Everything should be in writing. Always. Verbal agreements are nice, but paper protects you.

CHAPTER 11

FROM VINE TO VICTORY—YOU LANDED THE JOB, NOW WHAT?

Congratulations! You accepted the job. Take a moment. Really. After the long, emotional rollercoaster of job searching, rejections, and waiting games, you did it. You're no longer a job seeker. You're someone who landed the role. Let that sink in. Celebrate it. Own it. You can finally exhale.

Now it's time to shift gears. This next phase, your first few months on the job, is critical. It's where you lay the foundation, build trust, and start affirming that the company made the right choice by hiring you. Your new focus is proving you belong there.

This phase sets the tone for your reputation, growth trajectory, and how others perceive your potential. And yet, this is often where people fumble the ball. They let the excitement of landing the role distract them from what comes next: doing the work, showing up consistently, and laying the groundwork for long-term success.

No Champagne at Orientation, Just Calendars and Chaos

Rachel:

"It's so exciting when you get the job!! This is my favorite part of the process by far. Just seeing how happy people are, knowing that their hard work paid off. But here's the part no one posts on social media: the not-so-glamourous, actual working part. It's not always what you pictured at first, and that's okay. It might not look like the Nancy Meyers dream office, with a perfectly curated desktop and a boss who instantly becomes your mentor."

Lori:

"Instead, the reality could be a folding table next to the supply closet and a boss in back-to-back meetings who forgot you were even starting today. One minute you're the chosen one, the top candidate, and the next—you're being handed a laptop that still has someone else's desktop background."

Rachel:

"First day jitters are real. A new place, new people, new responsibilities to juggle, all while acting confident and as if you know what's going on. It's a lot. I don't think people give it enough credit. Starting a new job should be on the official list of life's most stressful events, right between moving and filing your taxes. Especially if you're anything like me and get a little socially anxious in unfamiliar situations."

Lori:

"The truth is that those first few months are extremely humbling in most cases. And that's exactly how it should be. You're not there to have all the answers—you're there to learn, stay curious, and prove they made the right call hiring you."

Rachel:

"It's not about being perfect. It's about being the person who listens and easily pivots even when the job is messier or more confusing than you pictured. So charge your laptop, bring your best attitude, and leave the ego at the door. You're not here to blend in, you're here to grow."

Let's break down how to thrive in this next phase and avoid the rookie mistakes that could cost you down the line.

The First Day: It's Showtime

Let's start with expectations. Your first day likely won't involve creative brainstorming sessions or being invited into high-level strategy meetings. You may spend time filling out HR forms, learning how to use the printer, or getting trained on the company's project management software. That's not a letdown—it's onboarding. And your ability to approach it with humility and eagerness will speak volumes.

You are now part of a bigger system. Think of your first week as a listening tour. Be the person who's curious, observant, and respectful. Resist the urge to make suggestions or "fix" things before you fully understand how they work. The best thing you can do is take notes, ask thoughtful questions, and express gratitude for every piece of insight someone offers you.

Early Roles Are Rarely Glamorous—and That's Okay

This is the part no one posts about on LinkedIn. You might find yourself answering phones all day, booking travel, building out calendars, creating spreadsheets, or sitting in on meetings just to take notes. It's not glamorous, and it might not feel like the job you imagined.

But here's the secret: that's exactly how it's supposed to be.

Every successful person you admire—in entertainment, business, tech, you name it—started out doing the less exciting work. They sharpened pencils, got coffee, transcribed calls, or cleaned up someone else's mess. That work might not have been thrilling, but it built the habits and instincts that made them indispensable later. So don't underestimate these small moments. Do them well, and people will trust you with more.

Patience Over Promotions

We live in a culture obsessed with speed, followers, titles, and status. But real career growth doesn't happen overnight. It unfolds quietly, over time, in moments when no one is watching. Real career growth comes from doing the work, again and again, even when it's boring or thankless.

If you're a few weeks into your new job and feeling impatient, that's normal. You might think, "I'm ready for more," or "Why am I doing this entry-level task?" But mastering the basics is the key to earning bigger responsibilities. Your job right now is to prove you can show up, deliver consistently, and be someone your team can count on.

That's how doors start to open. Not because you demanded a promotion, but because you quietly earned one.

Professionalism Is a Daily Choice

Now that you're in the door, how you carry yourself matters more than ever. Professionalism isn't just about wearing the right outfit or having a nice signature on your email (although, yes, please do both). It's about your attitude, your communication, your discretion, and your consistency.

To maintain professionalism, here are some quick rules to live by:

- **Be on time.** It's one of the simplest ways to show respect.
- **Keep your word.** If you say you'll do something, do it. On time and without needing reminders. Your boss wants to check this task off their list the minute they delegate it to you.
- **Don't overshare.** You don't need to tell your boss you're hungover or had a fight with your roommate. Keep boundaries.
- **Use professional language.** Emails are not texts. Skip the emojis and read everything twice before hitting send. Don't make careless spelling errors that could be avoided.
- **Own your mistakes.** You *will* mess up at some point. When you do, acknowledge it and fix it. That's how professionals grow.

Your job isn't just to get the work done…it's to be someone people want to work with. That reputation will carry you forward more than any degree or certification.

Build Real Relationships and be a Team Player

No matter what field you're in, your ability to build trust and connection with your team will define your career. You don't need to be the loudest voice in the room or the life of the office happy hour. But you do need to show up for others, collaborate, and treat everyone, yes, everyone, with respect.

Offer to help. Give credit. Ask thoughtful questions. Be someone who makes other people's jobs easier.

And remember: your reputation travels faster than you do. Especially in tight-knit industries, your behavior now might determine the next opportunity you get down the line.

Common First Job Mistakes (and How to Avoid Them)

- **Expecting constant praise.** You won't get a gold star for every task. Do it well anyway.
- **Talking more than listening.** You learn more with your ears than with your mouth.
- **Being too casual too fast.** Earn familiarity. Don't assume it.
- **Overpromising and underdelivering.** Always be realistic about your bandwidth.
- **Ghosting your boss or team.** Even if you're overwhelmed, disappearing is never the answer. Communicate.

Five Golden Rules to Succeed in Your First Role

1. Show up early. Stay late if needed. Be dependable.

2. Treat every task, no matter how small, like it matters (because it does).
3. Don't ask what the company can do for you. Ask what you can do for the team.
4. Take feedback as a gift, not a personal attack.
5. Be the person people trust—not just to get it done, but to get it done well.

Final Thought: You're Planting Seeds

Your career is like planting a garden. You water it every day. You pull the weeds. You show up and don't rush it. And one day, that tiny seed becomes something much bigger: a job you love, a mentor who invests in you, an unexpected opportunity you never saw coming. But none of that growth happens unless you commit to doing the work, especially when no one's clapping.

You got the job. Now earn it.

Five Takeaways for After You Landed the Job

1. **You're Not Done—You're Just Getting Started:** Getting hired is a milestone, not the finish line. Your reputation, work ethic, and attitude from this point forward are what truly shape your career.
2. **Small Tasks are Big Opportunities in Disguise:** How you handle the "boring" stuff—like scheduling, note-taking, and admin—signals how you'll handle larger responsibilities. Nail the basics.

3. **Professionalism Is Your Daily Currency:** Be reliable, discreet, respectful, and prepared. These qualities build trust and trust builds careers.
4. **Relationships Matter More Than Titles:** Be a team player. Ask questions. Offer help. Every interaction is a chance to earn respect and build your internal network.
5. **Growth Takes Time, But Effort Is Noticed:** You may not get a promotion tomorrow, but showing up with consistency and humility lays the groundwork for long-term success.

CHAPTER 12

THE NEXT VINTAGE—DON'T FEAR AI, FRIEND IT

Learn how to use AI to supercharge your job search, from résumés to interviews, while keeping the one thing technology can't replicate: your human edge.

AI is no longer just a buzzword; it's part of the modern job search, whether you realize it or not. From networking tools to mock interviews, AI is shaping how candidates search for work and how they are vetted and hired. Luckily, you don't have to be a tech wizard to take advantage of it. With the right tools and approach, you can make AI your secret weapon—not your stumbling block.

In this chapter, we break down specific, practical ways you can use AI to support your job hunt: from crafting compelling résumés to preparing for interviews and tracking your applications like a pro.

Don't Let the Bot Steal Your Thunder

Rachel:

"Using AI in your job search is like hiring a supersmart, slightly robotic assistant who never sleeps. The good news is, finally, someone actually reads your résumé line by line and never judges you."

Lori:

"AI can help you polish your résumé or assist in drafting the perfect thank-you note. What it can't capture is the way you light up when you talk about architecture, or the way you come alive when a company's mission actually means something to you. The human connection is the thing that makes you the most memorable. And no algorithm can fake that."

Rachel:

"AI also won't ever be able to replace your intuition, or your excellent taste or your natural charm and wit. That's what you bring to the table. Don't forget that *you* are the main character, not the machine!"

Let AI Work for You

Résumé Creation and Optimization

If your résumé hasn't been updated in over a year or is filled with vague buzzwords like "team player" or "go-getter," AI can help you fix that, *fast*.

How AI Helps:

- Tailor your résumé to each job description. Paste the job post into your preferred AI and ask, "Which skills and keywords should I highlight based on this job description?"
- Reword clunky bullet points. You can request: "Rewrite this to be more results-oriented: 'Helped plan marketing events.'"
- Fix formatting or grammar. Tools like AI can polish the entire document for tone and clarity.
- Highlight measurable impact. AI can help you add phrases like "resulted in a 20 percent increase in engagement" when prompted with the context.

Tip: Don't forget to feed AI the right inputs. The more details you give about what you actually did, the better your results.

Cover Letters, Thank-You Notes, and Outreach Emails

Writing a cover letter is often the most dreaded part of the application. AI can ease the pain by giving you a solid first draft to work with, helping you personalize your cover letter in a way that sounds like you.

How AI Helps:

- Generates a personalized cover letter based on your résumé and the job description.
- Suggests language for networking emails or recruiter outreach.
- Creates polished, professional thank-you notes after interviews.

Tip: Never send AI-generated text word-for-word without editing. When generating professional materials with AI, always go back and add your own voice. Those special touches are most likely the details that will stand out. Being too generic will not make the impression you want it to. There is just something about a personal touch that is unmatched.

Sample Prompt:

"I just interviewed for a Project Coordinator role at Warner Bros. We talked about my background in events and their need for logistics support. Can you help me write a thank-you email that reflects that?"

Interview Prep and Practice

AI can help you go into interviews more confident, more prepared, and more thoughtful about your responses.

How AI Helps:

- Creates mock interview questions based on the job description.
- Helps you structure your answers.
- Gives feedback on your tone and clarity (if used with voice-to-text or transcription tools).
- Simulates practice interviews using chatbot platforms.

Sample Prompt:

"I'm interviewing for a Sales Coordinator position. What are ten questions I might be asked, and how should I answer them?"

Job Search Organization and Tracking

Job hunting can get messy fast, especially when you're juggling multiple applications, follow-ups, and networking emails. AI can help keep your search structured.

How AI Helps:

- Organize job leads, application status, follow-ups, and due dates.
- Generate reminders for thank-you notes and interview prep.
- Summarize job descriptions so you can quickly compare roles or prep notes before applying.

Tip: Create an AI-powered "Job Tracker" template to keep everything organized—interviews, thank-you notes, and feedback—all in one easy-to-find place.

LinkedIn and Online Profile Optimization

AI can help make your professional online presence more compelling, which is critical when recruiters are Googling you.

How AI Helps:

- Writes your LinkedIn headline and "About" section based on your experience and goals.
- Suggests skills to add based on your résumé or job interests.
- Optimizes your LinkedIn profile for search algorithms (hello, recruiter visibility).
- Creates social content if you want to post about industry trends, job search updates, or personal wins.

Sample Prompt:

"Write a compelling LinkedIn 'About' section for a recent college grad with a degree in psychology, and interest in marketing and community engagement."

Skill Building and Career Mapping

Don't know what job titles match your skills? Not sure what you're missing to get to the next level? AI can help you figure that out, too.

How AI Helps:

- Suggests career paths based on your interests and education.
- Identifies skill gaps based on the jobs you want.
- Recommends online courses to fill those gaps.

Prompt Example:

"I want to become a Brand Strategist. What are five core skills I need, and what courses should I take to get started?"

Portfolio and Content Creation

If your field requires a portfolio, think design, writing, marketing, or media, AI can help you shape it.

How AI Helps:

- Generates a professional biography and concise case study blurbs for projects you've worked on.
- Refines your personal brand story for websites or online portfolios.
- Helps you design visually polished presentations in your own voice using the right tools.

Customized Job Alerts and AI-Powered Job Boards

Some job platforms now use AI to match you to roles based on your browsing and application history.

How AI Helps:

- Delivers better job matches based on your profile and skills.
- Alerts you to jobs early, sometimes before they're posted widely.
- Recommends roles you might not have considered, expanding your search.

AI Is a Tool—Not the Whole Toolbox

While AI can take a lot off your plate, the job search still requires your effort, judgment, and voice. AI won't build relationships for you. It doesn't beat that in-person, face-to-face connection needed for networking and long-term bonds. AI won't follow up with a recruiter, sit in an interview and smile with warmth, or answer a curveball question with grace.

AI will make things faster. It will make things easier. But it will never replace the most important part of the process: you.

Key Reminders for Using AI Responsibly:

- Always review, personalize, and proofread AI content before sending.
- Use AI for clarity and speed, not as a substitute for effort.
- Maintain your human tone in everything you write.
- Don't rely on AI to make decisions; use it to support your judgment.

- Stay updated. Digital tools evolve, and the field is changing rapidly.

Five Takeaways for Not Fearing AI, but Friending It

1. **AI Is Your Starting Line, Not Your Finish Line:** AI can draft your résumé, cover letter, and LinkedIn bio, but *you* still have to make your professional materials sound authentic.
2. **The Better Input, the Better Output:** Vague prompts get vague results. Give AI details and context if you want something worth using.
3. **Know When to Step In:** AI is great at summaries, structure, and tone cleanup. It's *not* great at understanding vibes, nuance, or when someone in the office is being passive-aggressively weird.
4. **Don't Skip the Review Step:** Don't be afraid to experiment, but always double-check. Don't blindly trust what it spits out. Always review and edit.
5. **No One Wants to Hire a Robot:** The real flex is combining AI efficiency with human charm. Because no one ever got hired for being the best robot in the room.

CHAPTER 13

FINAL SIPS, YOU'VE GOT THIS

So here you are. You made it to the end, and that means you now have a shiny new toolbox packed with everything you need to crush your job search. From where to find the best opportunities, to crafting a standout résumé, writing the kind of cover letter people actually read, nailing your interviews, handling rejection with resilience, and even becoming besties (not enemies) with AI. Now you've got the goods!

We didn't write this book to be another pile of vague advice you skim once and forget. This is your guidebook. Your cheat sheet. Your confidence boost. Come back to it any time you need a refresh or a reminder that you're not alone in this. You already have what it takes. You just needed help to package it, present it, and pitch it like a pro.

Now it's on you to commit. Follow the tips. Put in the effort. Trust your instincts. Be bold. Be real. Be relentless.

You are prepped. You are ready. You are fully capable of landing a job that aligns with your strengths, your values, and your goals. You've got this. Repeat "I am an OFFER MAGNET" to yourself daily until it becomes a reality.

And when in doubt? Reread this chapter before an interview. Take a breath. Remind yourself: You belong in the room.

We believe in you.

Now go out there and crush it.

A Note from Us to You

To everyone who picked up this book, whether you devour it in one weekend or dog-ear pages as you go, thank you. We wrote *Straight from the Grapevine* because we've seen what works, what doesn't, and what absolutely drives us crazy in the world of hiring, and we wanted to pass it on.

We know how stressful the job search can be. It can make you question your talent, your timing, and your whole life plan—especially when everyone else seems to be landing dream jobs on Instagram while you're refreshing your email for the fifth time.

But we're here to tell you: It's not about perfection. It's about progress, professionalism, and a little perspective.

Yes, your résumé matters. So does your interview game, your thank-you note, your networking strategy, and your ability to follow up without being overeager. But what matters most is *how* you show up—for others, for opportunities, and for yourself.

We've walked this road. We've taken the wrong jobs. Sent the wrong emails. Worn the wrong outfits to the right meetings. And yet, somehow, here we are running a company, helping people land life-changing roles, and still laughing (most days).

If there's one thing we hope you take away, it's this: You are your best asset. Your grit, your kindness, your ability to learn, pivot, and bounce back, that's the stuff that builds careers.

So keep going. Keep growing. Keep raising your hand, asking questions, and believing that something better is always around the corner…even if you can't see it yet.

And if you ever feel lost in the weeds again, come back to us at Grapevine. We'll be here.

Now go crush it. We're cheering you on!

Rachel and Lori
Co-Founders, Grapevine
Staffing Experts, Résumé Editors, Career Truth-Tellers,
and Forever in Your Corner

CHAPTER 14

A POUR FROM OUR HEART

Job Search Lingo, Unfiltered

Alumni Network
A group of graduates from the same school or program. Great for networking and job referrals.

Applicant Pool
The total amount of candidates who have applied for a specific job.

Apprenticeship
A hands-on training program under the guidance of an expert. Common in trades and growing in other fields like tech.

ATS (Applicant Tracking System)
Software used by employers to filter and sort résumés before a human sees them. It scans for keywords and formatting.

Background Check
A process where employers verify your criminal, work, driving, education, or credit history.

Benefits Package
Extras offered beyond salary, like health insurance, 401(k), vacation time, or commuter perks.

Branding (Personal Brand)
How you present yourself professionally—online, in person, and in materials like your résumé or portfolio.

Bridge Job
A temporary or less-than-ideal job that helps you transition to your next career goal.

Career Coach
A professional who helps you define your goals, strategy, and confidence during your job search.

Career Pivot
Changing careers or industries using your transferable skills rather than starting over.

Company Culture
The overall vibe, values, and behavior norms of a workplace.

Contract Role / 1099
A non-employee position where you handle your own taxes and typically don't get benefits.

Cover Letter
A short letter that introduces you and your interest in a role. Should add value beyond the résumé.

Culture Fit
How well your personality and work style align with the company's values and team dynamics.

Drag-and-Drop Résumé Builder
A tool that helps you build résumés quickly using templates.

Elevator Pitch
A thirty to sixty second summary of who you are and what you do. Perfect for networking moments.

Entry Point
Your first job or step into a new field or company.

Entry-Level
A job designed for someone starting their career, often with minimal experience required.

Freelance
Working on short-term or project-based assignments as a self-employed individual.

Full-Time / W-2
Traditional employment with benefits and taxes handled by the employer.

Ghosted (by Employer)
When a company stops replying during the hiring process with no explanation.

Hard Skills
Technical or teachable abilities, like coding, editing, or using Excel.

Hidden Job Market
Unlisted jobs filled through referrals, internal candidates, or recruiters.

Hybrid Role
A job split between remote work and in-office time.

Internship
A short-term role (usually for students or recent grads) that provides hands-on experience in a specific field. Internships can be paid or unpaid, full-time or part-time, and are often used to build your résumé, gain industry exposure, and make valuable connections. Sometimes, they even lead to full-time offers, so treat them like real jobs (because they are).

Interview Panel
Multiple interviewers meet with you at once, often from different departments.

Job Alignment
When a job matches up with who you are and where you want to go, not just in terms of skills but values, goals, lifestyle, and energy. It's the "does this feel right?" gut check, plus the logical checklist.

Job Board
A website where employers post job openings and candidates can apply.

Job Description (JD)
A document that outlines the responsibilities, skills, and qualifications for a role.

Job Hopper
A person who changes jobs frequently. Can look negative unless well-explained.

Job Shadowing
Observing a professional in their role to learn more about the field.

Keywords
Important words in job descriptions that should appear in your résumé/cover letter.

LinkedIn
A professional networking platform used to job search, build your brand, and connect with others.

Mentor
A trusted advisor who provides career guidance, support, and feedback.

Networking
Building professional relationships that can lead to opportunities or advice.

Networking Call / Informational Interview
A casual conversation with someone in your field of interest to learn and build connections.

Offer Letter
A written confirmation of your job offer, including terms like salary and start date.

Onboarding
The process of getting you set up and trained in a new role.

Open Role / Opening
A position that's currently available and accepting applications.

Outreach Email
An email you send to make a connection or express interest in a job or industry.

Part-Time
A role that involves fewer hours than full-time, often with less or no benefits.

Portfolio
A collection of your best work samples to showcase your skills, especially in creative industries.

Portfolio Career
A career composed of multiple gigs, freelance roles, or part-time jobs rather than one full-time job.

Probation Period
A trial period when starting a new job where performance and fit are evaluated.

Red Flag
A warning sign that something about a job, company, or process might be off.

Referrals
Recommendations or introductions from people you know, often leading to faster interviews.

Remote Work
A job you can do from anywhere, as the role is not tied to a physical office.

Resignation Letter
A formal letter letting your employer know you're leaving your job.

Résumé
A one to two page document summarizing your experience, skills, and accomplishments.

Salary Range
The span of pay offered for a role. This is helpful context for knowing your value and negotiating.

Side Hustle
A job or gig you do outside your main role to earn extra income or explore interests.

Soft Skills
People skills—like communication, teamwork, or time management—that help you succeed at work.

STAR Method
A way to answer interview questions: Situation, Task, Action, Result.

Staffing Agency / Recruiter
A service or person who helps match candidates with job openings.

Talent Acquisition
Another term for recruiting; it is often used in HR departments.

Temp Job
A short-term role, often arranged by a staffing agency.

Transferable Skills
Skills that can be applied across roles or industries, like writing or project management.

Values Alignment
When your values and a company's mission or culture match up.

Work Sample / Test Project
An assignment or project you're asked to complete to demonstrate your skills.

OUR ACKNOWLEDGMENTS

Writing this book was a true labor of love, and it wouldn't have been possible without the incredible people who supported us along the way. First, thank you to the Grapevine community. To every student, job seeker, and dreamer who has ever wondered how to begin, this book is for you. Your trust and partnership fuel our purpose. Making the perfect match is still pure magic. Together, we've built more than careers, we've built a community. We want to thank our team for believing in us from day one and for guiding us through this process along the way: Jen Cohen (Agent), Anthony Ziccardi (Publisher at Post Hill Press), Aleigha Koss (Publishing Director at Post Hill Press), Rachel Paul (Editor), Sarah Hall and Hailey Helms (Publicists at SHP), Carolyn Joyce and Joshua Elliot (Social Media at SHP), Paula Marshall (Photographer), and Brittney Cunningham (Tech and Website Queen). Thank you to the amazing Sharon Abbring for being our domestic goddess and for Chloe Schmitz for your creativity and overall vibes.

Lori's Acknowledgments

To my beloved children, Sascha and Addison, thank you for your patience and for inspiring me every day to work hard and dream big to do better for you. To my husband, Jeff Briller: You've held it all together with strength, humor, and love. I couldn't do any of this without you.

Your unwavering belief in me gives me the courage to keep going. To my dad, Howard Zuker, and Nancy: Dad, you planted the seed of self-belief early, and Nancy, you've always understood my drive. Thank you both for everything. Your guidance and support have been the foundation of my journey. To my mom and Barry: Mom, your work ethic shaped me, and Barry, your quiet strength has always grounded me. I'm forever grateful. You both taught me that showing up with integrity is the greatest success. To Pamela Robinson, you gave me my start in this business and taught me what it means to lead with strength and savvy, so thank you. Your mentorship has left an imprint that continues to guide me. To my friends, thank you for loving me through every season—even when I vanish—and for always showing up. Your steady presence reminds me I'm never alone, no matter how full life gets. To Alyson Mazer, your legacy lives in everything I do. Thank you for showing me the heart and hustle behind this work. I carry your spirit into every conversation, placement, and win. To Rachel Zaslansky Sheer, my partner in business and life chaos. You're the yin to my yang, and I wouldn't want to do any of this without you. Your brilliance, loyalty, heart, and humor have made the ride unforgettable.

Rachel's Acknowledgments

Thank you to my husband Noah Sheer for the unconditional love and for always supporting my wildest dreams. Leave it to us! None of this would be possible without you by my side. To Griffin Samson Sheer, please continue feeding me with your delicious dishes, silly jokes, and cuddles galore. I am so proud of the exceptional young man you have become. I love you to the moon and *no* back. Hazel Ayla Sheer, continue being the star of our lives and keep dreaming big with your pool and balcony and all the puppies, horses and chocolate in the world. The world is your stage and I love you beyond words. To my Dad, Sheldon Zaslansky, thank you for inspiring me and showing me what a true boss looks like, and for your invaluable advice and perspective. You truly know everything about everything! Beth Sheer, thank you for always making me laugh and all of your advice for almost two decades and counting. Jeff Briller, thank you for all the things you do behind the scenes. You are the GOAT. ABS—may we live parallel lives forever. Thank you for all your wisdom, good vibes, and constant support. You're next! To all my amazing friends and family from the east and west, I am so lucky to have such a solid support system. You've cheered me on from the sidelines and I am forever grateful to be surrounded by such strong, smart, and quality people. Lastly, my work wife, Lori Zuker Briller, you are my soul sister for life, and I love you beyond words. Thank you for doing life and business with me every day.

ABOUT THE AUTHORS

Photo Credit: Paula Marshall

Rachel Zaslansky Sheer and Lori Zuker Briller are seasoned recruiters and co-founders of TheGrapevineAgency.com, a leading talent recruitment agency they have successfully run together for over twenty years. Drawing from extensive experience across multiple industries, they have witnessed firsthand the common mistakes that hold candidates back in the job search. Their passion for empowering young people led them to co-author *Straight from the Grapevine: How to Crush Your Job Search*, a practical guide designed to equip high school and college students with the tools and confidence to launch successful careers.

Lori graduated from the University of Wisconsin, and Rachel from the University of Maryland. Both are committed to mentoring the next generation of professionals and are recognized for their candid, down-to-earth advice.